THE CASH FLOW
REAL ESTATE AGENT

Praise for *The Cash Flow Real Estate Agent*

"Dear George,

I am pleased to inform you that you have been chosen as the Life Enrichment Instructor of the Year by Continuing Education at Kennesaw State University. This is a truly unique honor, and I'd like to offer my sincere congratulations.

Each year, Continuing Education at KSU recognizes faculty who have gone 'above and beyond' in pursuit of excellence. You clearly share our passion to make a difference in our community. With your help, students are creating new opportunities personally and professionally. They are making dreams come true and eliminating obstacles. We are proud to be part of these accomplishments and congratulate you for the important role you play in supporting Continuing Education."

—Testimonial from Barbara S. Calhoun, dean of Continuing Education at Kennesaw State University, where George Ansong was an adjunct instructor of real estate investments for about ten years

"We did four deals. As early as 2000 and as late as 2019. Total of all deals: $426K. The deals were: two on Jernigan Drive, Atlanta. One on Nelms Street. One on Old Briar Court. In each case I remember George visited the property, reviewed the progress, made recommendations, offered input, and followed up at the end of the project.

We looked at several other deals but did not fit my 'winning formula' as George calls it.

I think the best benefit I got from my years of association with George is that he has always been there. Unlike others, who seem to dibble and dabble in real estate, he has remained in the business and seems to always try to find an angle. The other quality I find in George is untrainable and does not necessarily come with time nor experience: it is his unwavering positive attitude. Every time I speak to George, he has an upbeat and optimistic disposition about the market place and the opportunities that can be gleaned.

My total property value is about $1.6 million."

—John an investor from Atlanta, Georgia

"As an investor who has worked with George over the years, I enjoyed working with one of the most experienced, knowledgeable, and passionate real estate agents in Atlanta.

Within the last year (2020–2021) we have closed two great deals worth $540,000, and today those deals are worth over $700,000. As an investor, I would say your real estate agent experience matters. I have been lucky to work with George. All the deals I have worked with George I have managed to walk into a minimum of $50,000 in equity, and with today's market, we managed to buy in excellent locations.

George is my resource guide. I love working with him because he understands the Atlanta and surrounding markets, and has perfect real estate investment strategy.

George is the kind of agent that you call or text any time and you are sure you will get a response. I call him my real estate agent. 'My George' an agent who became family.

Total value of my real estate portfolio is $1 million and I see $10 million in a near future with George."

— Allan from Atlanta, Georgia

"Working with George has been a true example of a professional real estate investor. He understands the market and has an intimate knowledge of the area we operate and property values. We are a buy, renovate, and sell company. Over the past two years, we have bought and renovated over $2.5 million worth of real estate. It's great to work with George. He is very knowledgeable, very reassuring, and has a very positive outlook in life."

— D. H. – EDC Group

THE CASH FLOW
REAL ESTATE AGENT

A Step-by-Step Guide
to Working with Investors

George Ansong

Asempa Enterprises Inc
Atlanta, GA

ISBN: 979-8-9852618-0-6 - Paperback
eISBN: 979-8-9852618-1-3 - eBook

Library of Congress Control Number: 2021922821

Printed in the United States of America   1 1 1 6 2 1

⊚This paper meets the requirements of ANSI/NISO Z39.48-1992 (Permanence of Paper)

Cover by: Scot Mmobuosi

To my wife, Vena Ansong, who has patiently stood by my side all these years. You are a true gem and a trooper. I love you with an everlasting love.
My children: Shawn, Eric, Jessica (Yaayaa), Kwabena (Kobi)—You are the best—continue to strive for the best!
Grandchildren: Cedric, Alaysia, Colin, Ashton, Erin— Always know that the sky is the limit.
My late mother, Janet Yeboah, for keeping an eye on my first, faltering steps.

"The cave you fear to enter holds the treasure you seek."
—*Joseph Campbell*

Contents

Introduction
About the Cash Flow
Real Estate Agent

Cash flow is the net cash and cash equivalents needed to transfer into and out of a business. Cash received represents inflows, while money spent represents outflows. As agents, we should position ourselves to take advantage of real estate investment—not as agents, but as investors. Understanding the concept of cash flow will allow us to manage our business to acquire more investment properties for our portfolio.

You can increase cash flow with income-producing property and good management—we know that an income-producing property will give you income consistently. It is possible to increase the cash flow from a property that you have acquired: you can establish good price controls, increase rent regularly, develop other sources of income, and manage your property very well. Not only can you increase your income with investment properties but you will be able to do many flip deals that will improve your capital position tremendously.

The Cash Flow Real Estate Agent focuses on the different real estate investment strategies that agents can employ to expand their cash flow position but also acquire the mindset to work with investors. It is a step-by-step guide designed to help real estate agents exponentially increase their production and income by effectively working with real estate investors.

The book encourages real estate agents to buy income-producing properties for their portfolios and minimize their dependence on sporadic commission checks.

The book is packed with strategies, techniques, and insights to make the reader's income and production take off.

The book represents many decades of real estate investment, mentoring, and coaching.

In this step-by-step guide, you will learn how to:

- work with real estate investors to exponentially grow your business and income
- develop the wealth-building mindset
- reassess your competitive edge in the industry
- understand the two basic real estate investment models
- ask when working with real estate investors to help you identify their working strategies
- identify exit strategies in your investment toolbox
- identify the ten common mistakes that real estate investors make and how to avoid them

1

The Commission Check and the Agent —Time to Build Your Own Empire

While real estate investors are buying properties, generating cash flow, and making big money by flipping properties, most real estate agents have to make do with periodic commission checks.

Agents have many advantages working in the industry. But one disadvantage is that nobody teaches agents how to seize the opportunities they encounter every day in their professional lives. Agents come across all kinds of deals—from a seller facing foreclosure to people confronting such circumstances as divorce, illness, moving, or making two mortgage payments. People with all these issues need a helping hand.

The real estate agent has some advantages over the real estate investor.

Agents:

- are licensed by the state and have to comply with numerous regulations. They are familiar with the MLS—Multiple Listing Service—in their area. The MLS is a vital tool.
- know CMA—Comparable Market Analysis
- know about inspections and due diligence

1

- know real estate contracts intimately
- know contractors, fixer-uppers, and repair people
- know attorneys and title companies
- are familiar with negotiation inside and out
- know many vendors in the real estate industry: surveyors, appraisers
- know service companies such as home warranty and home inspection
- know mortgage companies that are familiar with loan programs
- are aware of all available loan programs
- are intimate with the real estate market, market trends, and are abreast of the current markets
- know how to work with buyers and sellers
- know the psychology of the typical buyer and seller
- know how to list and sell properties
- know about staging properties to get them sold

The typical new agent is exposed to the many facets of representing buyers and sellers within a short time—but not a lot about real estate investing.

Most brokerage companies emphasize listing and selling; their continuing education programs teach agents to sell or list more properties. From the brokerage company's point of view, and understandably so, it is not in their interest to have their agents investing in real estate. My recommendation is for agents to go elsewhere for real estate investment education and knowledge. Then they can invest in their own real estate portfolios.

As all agents know, our business is very cyclical. There will be times when there is a lull in your production that might affect cash flow.

So, how do you manage those instances if you don't have any other income streams?

Agents have to think big and learn how to start limited liability companies, S-Corporations—entities structured to hold their assets to minimize their tax liability. Agents also can pool resources to buy commercial properties such as apartment complexes, strip malls, warehouses, or storage houses. Agents can also form syndicates and raise money to buy all kinds of investment properties. Opportunities include creating syndicates to raise money to purchase investment properties, networking with investors, and partnering with them to buy, rehab, and flip residential properties. All these activities will help multiply their income and assets.

Most brokerage companies do not offer any kind of retirement income. Real estate agents must learn how to invest in real estate and reap all its benefits: income, depreciation, appreciation, and leverage.

Lessons from the iBuyer: Disruptions in the Real Estate Industry

An iBuyer is a real estate company that will make an instant offer on a house, buy it at less than market value, fix the home, and put it back on the market. Examples of iBuyers on the market are Offerpad, Opendoor, Zillow, Knock, Redfin, We Buy Ugly Houses.

As agents and brokerage companies sat idly by, working on the old business model that I believe is not sustainable, iBuyers entered the marketplace with a vengeance with billions of dollars and started disrupting the real estate industry. The business model of the brokerage company is solely to teach agents how to represent buyers and sellers, recruit more agents to the brokerage companies, and work on the commission splits; there is no education on the fundamentals of real estate investing.

Just think about this: The typical iBuyer is an investor who buys a piece of property under value, repairs the property, and lists the property for sale. This same iBuyer acts as an investor and becomes a brokerage company by listing and selling the property that it acquired and fixed.

Individual agents can adopt the iBuyer's business model just by becoming more familiar with real estate investment. The typical agent can form a partnership with other agents and operate the same business model as the typical iBuyer.

Once again, remember that an iBuyer is not only an investor but also a brokerage company; that is their business model, and that is how they are disrupting the real estate market in a tremendous and impactful way!

We have to start thinking like an investor with a purpose—to invest in properties and create cash flow.

Building Wealth Quickly

Agent's balance sheet (pre-investment)

Assets (What You Own)		Liabilities (What You Owe)	
Cash:	$7,980	Credit Card:	$5,980
Personal Home:	$250,000	Mortgage:	$200,000
Auto:	$25,000	Auto loan:	$9,000
Assorted Personal		Assorted Bills:	$8,700
Belongings:	$10,000		
Total Assets:	$292,980	Total Liabilities:	$223,680

NET WORTH $292,980 − $223,680 = $69,300

Agent's balance sheet (post-investment)

Assets		Liabilities	
Cash:	$17,980	Credit Card:	$5,980
Auto:	$25,000	Auto:	$9,000
Personal Property:	$350,000	Mortgage:	$200,000
Duplex:	$450,000	Mortgage:	$190,000
Duplex:	$550,000	Mortgage:	$395,000
Total Assets:	$1,392,950	Total Liabilities:	$799.980

NET WORTH $1,392,950 − $799,980 = $592,970

NOTE: Every real estate agent should be doing a net-worth analysis; all should pledge to increase their net worth every two years.

My Observation

Appreciation is the real estate investor's best friend, so investing almost always adds to your net worth. We have to break our cycle of dependence on commission income, replacing or supplementing it with passive cash flow, which also reduces tax liability.

Ways Agents Can Minimize Their Dependence on the Commission Check:

1. Take real estate investment courses.
2. Read books on real estate investment.
3. Join a local real estate investment association.
4. Network with other investors.
5. Select like-minded real estate investors to form an investment club.
6. Hire a coach or a mentor to guide you in your investment activities.
7. Set aside 15 percent of your commission check— devote it to real estate investment.
8. Form a Limited Liability Company or Sub Chapter S-Corp to run your real estate investment business and minimize your tax liabilities.
9. Buy your first real estate investment property; repeat the process every two years.
10. Work with real estate investors as a way to learn from them.
11. Establish a relationship with real estate attorneys who work with investors.
12. Get to know accountants who also work with real estate investors.
13. Become familiar with private money lenders.
14. Meet hard money or private lenders in the industry.
15. Learn about foreclosure investing.
16. Learn how to raise money to do real estate deals.

17. Learn creative real estate financing.
18. Start a library of real estate books (recommendations are on page 125).
19. Join real estate investment groups on social media.
20. Join BiggerPockets—an online real estate education company.
21. Network with other agents who are investors.
22. Join REI-USA—an online platform that teaches real estate investment.
23. Listen to podcasts on real estate investment.

2

The Mindset of the
Real Estate Investor

C ertain beliefs, habits, and behaviors separate the wealthy from the rest of the world. Having a wealth mindset will guide you to make the most of the money you have. A wealth mindset means spending less, making wise investments, and looking for ways to improve your financial standing with minimal risk.

For example, to many, an abandoned property is an eyesore. But someone with a wealth mindset will be thinking about acquiring the property at a minimum price, fixing the property, and selling it for big money. Even if one does not have the money, he will think of ways to partner with somebody to acquire the property.

There's another keyword: paradigm—or looking at something or a situation in a different way. Real estate agents have to change their paradigms about working with real estate investors.

Always remember that our paradigms influence our perception. Acquiring investors as clients would require you to change your perceptions about investors. For example, the popular misconception is that investors want to submit low-ball offers. That is a myth! Investors want to make offers that dovetail with their investment strategies. Knowing the investment strategy of the investor will dispel this erroneous perception.

Our paradigms also can influence how we manage our time.

Our productivity and income will grow exponentially as we master "activity management" instead of time management. We need to change our paradigms to realize that time is a resource and a treasure and should be treated as such.

There are two kinds of wealth:

1. Visible Wealth: that which we can see with the naked eye, such as buildings, equipment, vehicles, possessions.
2. Invisible Wealth: natural talent, skills, relationships, talents, honesty, time, intelligence, experience, habits, ideas, integrity. Some examples: the ability to put deals together and the ability to raise capital for investment activities.

I believe we concentrate too much on the visible wealth; everyone can see, for example, our expensive home or vehicle.

But the talent given to us at birth or acquired over the years is essential—we need it to help build our invisible wealth. My experience as a real estate investor and instructor helped me to partner with investors who needed my expertise to guide them. I partnered with several investors, and we acquired numerous properties. But my partners provided most of the capital to fund almost all such properties.

Ways to Develop a Wealth-Building Mentality

1. Education: Take short, focused courses emphasizing real estate investment or entrepreneurship. Many of such courses are offered on such websites as biggerpockets.com. Most states have real estate associations that you can join for a small fee. REI–USA is a credible online real estate education platform you can join. The continuing education departments of many colleges and universities also offer inexpensive real estate investment courses.

2. Mentoring: Find a coach to guide and encourage you.
3. Books: Read up on real estate investing. (There is a list at the end of this book.)
4. Make mistakes: This sounds counter-intuitive, but mistakes are a great learning tool; do not let your fear of them keep you from achieving your goals.
5. Operate with an investor mentality, one of finding opportunities and capitalizing on them.
6. Dream big, but be flexible in the details and use your imagination.
7. Learn to apply leverage: Leverage is what separates those who achieve wealth from those who don't. You can't reach the goal by trading time for money, and you can't do it all yourself. You need leverage.
8. Learn how to manage your money—this is an acquired skill.
9. Learn to build a supportive environment that reinforces your wealth-building mentality.
10. Live with integrity: This is non-negotiable. No amount of money can replace a good night's sleep, a clear conscience, and a peaceful mind.
11. Start thinking like an investor.
12. Learn how to make money work for you.
13. Learn how to take calculated risks.

3

Understanding the Numbers of Real Estate Investment

I n real estate investing, the numbers tell the story.

Investors look at properties from a different perspective than your ordinary buyer—the investor looks at the numbers, while emotions drive the everyday buyer.

This is why agents, when listing a property for a potential buyer, have to make sure the property looks appealing: we have to de-clutter, de-personalize, de-neutralize, and play up the curb appeal. It's all to appeal to the buyer's emotions. I can understand why buyers buy emotionally before they justify it logically.

Contrast this to the typical investor. Investors will look at the strategy they are adopting from the beginning: are they buying to rent or rehab and sell?

It can be frustrating to work with investors if you don't understand their mindset. Investors are not interested in the gorgeous house on the corner or the house with all the sizzling features. For the rehab investor, very often, the uglier the property, the better.

To succeed as a real estate investor, you must analyze potential investments and look at the numbers. Here are eight real estate numbers of which you must be aware.

1. Capitalization Rates (Cap Rate)

The capitalization rate measures the rate of return on the income you receive before debt service based on the total price you have paid for the property. To determine the capitalization rate of a property, simply divide the net annual operating income before debt service by the total price paid for the property.

Capitalization Rate = Net Operating Income Before Debt Service / Purchase Price

The Capitalization Rate: Often called the cap rate, this is the ratio of Net Operating Income (NOI) to property asset value. So, for example, if a property recently sold for $1 million and had an NOI of $100,000, then the cap rate would be $100,000/$1,000,000, or 10 percent.

$$\frac{\text{Net Operating Income}}{\text{Total Price of the Asset}} \times 100\%$$

$$\frac{13,200}{100,000} = 13.2\%$$

NOTE: This is an attractive rate for any income property. Typical capitalization rate ranges from the low 9 percent to 12 percent.

2. Return on Investment.

ROI measures the profit of an investment as a percentage of the cost of that investment. To calculate for real estate, you can include all the advantages of real estate investment to measure the effectiveness of your investment. This includes appreciation, tax advantages, depreciation allowance, and of course, income from the property itself.

Your ROI is much higher when you obtain a mortgage to buy your property—the more leverage, the higher your ROI.

The ROI on rental property varies because it depends on whether the property is financed in cash or through a mortgage. Generally, the less cash used for a down payment on the property, the larger the mortgage loan balance will be, but the greater your ROI. Conversely, the more cash paid upfront and the less you borrow, the lower your ROI because your initial cost would be higher. In other words, financing allows you to boost your ROI in the short term because your initial costs are lower.

Return on Investment = Net Profit

$$\text{Return on Investment} = \frac{\text{Net Profit}}{\text{Cost of Investment}} \times 100\%$$

3. Cash-On-Cash Return.

As an investor, you should be concerned with the cash flow from your rental property. When you divide your cash flow by the amount of cash you put down on the property, you get the cash-on-cash return figure. Note that this cash-on-cash rate is computed after you have paid your mortgage and all other expenses. Use the net income of the investment to measure the cash-on-cash return.

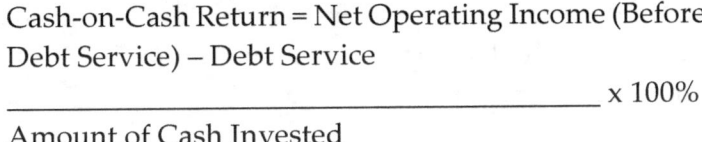

$$\text{Cash-on-Cash Return} = \frac{\text{Net Operating Income (Before Debt Service)} - \text{Debt Service}}{\text{Amount of Cash Invested}} \times 100\%$$

Return on Investment vs. Cash-on-Cash

Cash-on-cash return measures how much cash an investment property will generate, whereas Return of Investment measures the total wealth of the investment. (Total wealth includes appreciation, depreciation, and income.)

4. The annual percentage constant.

This measurement tells you what percentage of the original amount of money borrowed is required to cover interest and principal (total amount borrowed). The typical annual constant is between 9 percent and 12 percent.

To calculate the annual percentage constant, divide the yearly amount of money you are paying for debt service by the amount of money financed.

> 9%–12%. On a typical $80,000 mortgage the annual percentage constant for debt service would be:

> 800 x 12 = $9,600 (Annual Payments)
> Amount Financed (Mortgage) = $80,000
> Therefore, Annual Percentage Constant =
> $80,000/$9,600 = 12%

This compares favorably with typical constants for such properties, which range between 9 percent and 12 percent.

5. The Loan-to-Value (LTV) Ratio.

Loan-to-Value Ratio is an assessment of lending risk that financial institutions and other lenders examine before approving a mortgage. Typically, loan assessments with high LTV ratios are considered higher-risk loans.

$$\text{Loan-to-value ratio} = \frac{\text{Mortgage Amount}}{\text{Property Value}}$$

For example, if you buy a home at $200,000, and make a $20,000 down payment, you will borrow $180,000. This results in an LTV ratio of 90% ($180,000/$200,000).

6. Debt Service Ratio.

The investor's ability to repay the debt obligation based on the property's income and performance.

For example, let's say the income from the property is $1,200, and the Principle, Interest, Taxes, and Insurance (PITI) comes to $900—Debt Coverage Ratio will be:

Income / Principal Interest Taxes Insurance (PITI)

$$\frac{\$1,200}{\$900} = 1.33$$

This means the property makes enough income to service its debt obligation. Lenders prefer a debt coverage factor of 1.2 or higher.

7. Gross Rent Multiplier.

GRM is used to calculate the potential profitability of similar properties in the same market based on the gross annual rental income.

GRM = Price/Gross Annual Rent

To calculate the Gross Rent Multiplier, divide the fair market value of a property by the annual gross rental income.

Price of property = $200,000
Gross Annual Rent = $2,700 x 12 = $32,400
$200,000 /$32,400 = 6.17

Typically, a GRM between 4 and 7 is considered "good" for a rental property. Again, it is important to note that a healthy GRM is dependent on your local market and its comparable properties.

8.   Gross Operating Income.

Determine GOI by subtracting the estimated annual losses due to non-payment or vacancies.

Let's assume our Gross Potential Income is $85,000. It is if all units are full, and all rents paid.

Based on experience, the current market, and rental occupancy, we estimate that our losses due to vacancies and non-payment will be 7 percent.

$85,000 x 7% = $5,950
$85,000 - $5,950 = $79,050 for our Gross Operating Income

How to Analyze a Rental Property Investment

1.   Determine monthly income (gross income)

This will be rent the current tenants are paying (visit www.rentometer.com to determine the rent for your area.)

2.   Calculate the monthly operating expenses

These may include property taxes, insurance, property management fees, mortgage or financing costs, and homeowner's association fees. Vacancy and repairs are key factors too. Expenses can include:

Property taxes: You can request from your local tax office (Realtor).
Insurance: Get a quote from an insurance provider.
Property management company fee: Usually about 10 percent of the monthly rent.
Utilities: Ask the previous owner for bill estimates to

get a rough idea of your expected monthly expenses. Of course, if tenants will pay utilities, you don't need to include this in your equation.

Homeowners Association fees: Sometimes, HOA fees can be tough to determine. The seller or agent may know the number already—but if not, you will have to call the neighborhood's HOA. If you only know the annual fee, divide it by twelve.

Vacancy: Figure on 10 percent of the monthly rent toward vacancy expenses.

Repairs: Again, this is an estimate, but it should not be left out. You can conservatively use between 5 percent and 15 percent of the rent roll percent depending on the property's condition.

3. Subtract the monthly expenses from the monthly rent

This is your net income—your monthly cash flow.
It can be either negative or positive, depending on the numbers.

4. Calculate the returns

The cap rate and the cash-on-cash return are two measures you need to calculate to determine the effectiveness of your return on investment (ROI).

A cap rate is simply the Net Operating Income (NOI) of a property divided by its purchase price. When analyzing an investment, the cap rate is a vital metric because it provides insight into the future. The cap rate is almost like an investor's crystal ball to predict the upcoming years.

Cash-on-cash return measures the profitability of investment properties by taking into account the financing methods.

Cash flow Analysis

A.	Asking Price	$100,000
B.	Down Payment	$20,000
C.	Mortgage Needed	$80,000
D.	Monthly Mortgage	$800
E.	No. of Units for Rent	1
F.	Monthly Rent	$1,200
G.	Yearly Income	$13,200 (1200 x 11)
H.	Less Annual Expenses	$ 9,600 (800 x 12)
I.	Net Gain (Net Income)	$3,600
J.	Rate of Return (ROI)	about 18%

Net Income/Money Invested = Rate of Return
$3,600/$20,000   18%

Appreciation, in general terms, is an increase in the value of an asset. Increases can occur for several reasons, including increased demand or weakening supply, or as a result of changes in inflation or interest rates.

FIVE-YEAR PROJECTED ANALYSIS OF APPRECIATION
Year 1 $100.000_____
Year 2 $105,000_____
Year 3 $110,000_____
Year 4 $115,000_____
Year 5 $120,000_____

FORMULA TO LIVE BY:
Market Value + Appreciation
    $120,000_____
Minus Existing Mortgage
    $100,000_____
Equals Current Equity
    $20,000_____

Do a five-year projection to visualize how you can begin to build your wealth.

4

Maximize Your Time with Investors Using the 80–20 Rule

"The wisdom of life consists in the elimination of non-essentials."

—Lin Yutang

A principle developed by Italian economist Vilfredo Pareto suggests 20 percent of your activities will account for 80 percent of your results. It is one of the most helpful concepts for life and time management.

Investors are repeat buyers, and you can make money from both the front end and back end. In the front end, you can help the investor acquire the property; the back end occurs when you help the investor sell the property. You can also partner with an investor and buy, rehab, and sell properties. Investors are known to do multiple deals per month—and you can be the agent helping them accomplish their goals.

There are an estimated twenty-eight million real estate investors in the US, and seven million claim to be active investors. The topic of real estate investment interests many people today, especially with a plethora of investment real estate reality shows on TV.

A survey found that 39 percent of active investors intend to increase their purchases in the next twelve months. About 65 percent, or 4.5 million, investors plan to buy the same or increase their investments. According to the National Association of Realtors, investors purchased 1.23 million homes, a 64.5 percent increase over previous years.

One in eight American adults consider themselves residential real estate investors or own residential investment property. Those 28.1 million people can be classified as follows: 3 percent or seven million people consider themselves to be real estate investors and an additional 9 percent of all American adults own investment properties today, according to the study. According to available statistics compiled by BiggerPockets—an online real estate website for real estate investors: a knowledgeable and talented real estate agent would be a valuable team member for a real estate investor. Still, you have to improve your skills as an investor-friendly agent and understand the mind of an investor. The synergy between an investor and a skilled agent could be exponential. You as an agent help investors acquire the property and then assist them in listing and selling the property. As an agent, you bring valuable skills to the table.

Many of the activities that an agent performs daily are probably wasted time. By focusing on the 20 percent of the actions that provide the most results, we can free up significant amounts of time to do the kind of things we want to do. When you work with real estate investors, it is not unusual to close multiple deals quickly, thus increasing your productivity and income.

5

The 11 Benefits of
Working with an Investor

M ost investors do not have the time or patience to deal with
a real estate agent who isn't an investor or doesn't have
some experience dealing with investors. There's too much at stake
for a novice real estate agent to make mistakes during the negotiation, contract, or due-diligence phase. It is interesting to note that
there are many benefits to working with an investor.

1.   **You earn front- and back-end fees:**

You help your investor clients buy and sell the property—and
you earn your commission on both ends of the transaction. If you
locate a potential buyer during the listing phase, your fees can
grow further.

2.   **You can form partnerships with investors:**

You can partner with an investor and do a 60 percent/40 percent
partnership—or whatever arrangement you agree on. You can set
up a limited liability company with an investor, acquire a property,
fix and sell it, and split the profit. You can acquire a multi-family or
commercial property with your investment partner for asymmetric

gain. Of course, as an agent, you have to disclose any interest in the property to your broker and potential buyers during resale.

3. You can do multiple deals with investors:

Serious investors do multiple deals, and are always looking to buy and sell.

4. You can do quick closings with investors:

Investors also do quick cash closings in seven to twenty-one days. Most of these properties' titles have been cleared already. Also, closing attorneys who regularly work with investors know how to move the closing file along and close the deals quickly.

5. You understand the mindset of the investor:

To facilitate this, pick their brains on how they analyze properties and learn their various investment strategies.

6. You understand all the nuances involved in a real estate investment:

Experienced investors come to the table with a lot of knowledge. As an agent aspiring to work with investors, learn as much as you can and attend as many real estate seminars as possible.

7. You understand all the financing options available to the real estate investor:

The ability to understand all the financing options available to the investor is crucial. This knowledge should include nontraditional financing, such as owner financing, subject-to financing, contract for deed, and wraparound mortgages.

8. You become a resource center to the investor:

As an agent, you expand your base of knowledge as far as real estate investment is concerned. You know how to conduct a Comparable Market Analysis (CMA), negotiate, understand contracts, the due-diligence process, and work with the numerous parties involved in a typical real estate transaction. You also understand the real estate market and the trends.

9. You become knowledgeable and understand the numbers involved in a real estate transaction:

With investors, no emotions are attached to the property. Decisions become automatic for example: capitalization rate; price appreciation in the area; income potential of a piece of property; wholesale price analysis; possible equity; return on investment (ROI); cash-on-cash return; cash flow analysis; and after repair value (ARV). These are the flavors that attract real estate investors.

10. You receive referrals from your investors:

Especially if you do a great job, investors—who have excellent connections in the community—will refer other investors to you.

11. You receive free investment advice from your investor:

You learn from real estate experiences—and you get paid to work them. You learn how investors negotiate, analyze property, and the kind of financing they use. Understanding how an investor thinks, strategizes, and plans is essential if you desire to work with investors. As agents, our knowledge never ends. We are always learning!

My Observation

More agents need to work with investors. Do that by attending the numerous real estate investor meetings, networking opportunities, and meet-ups.

6

The Fundamentals of
Real Estate Investment

The acronym IDEAL can explain the value of real estate investment:

I is for Income—the gross income derived from the rental of the property. You also can create an income stream through a wraparound mortgage, land contract, or lease option.

There are three kinds of income:

Passive—income from real estate, royalties, residual income
Portfolio—income from stock investments, dividends, etc.
Earned—income from a regular job or commission income

D is for Depreciation—a loss in real estate value brought about by a property's age, physical deterioration, or functional or economic obsolescence. Tax laws permit you to take a paper loss, although the value of your property is going up.

E is for Equity—the difference between the market value of the property and the amount the owner still owes on the mortgage. It is the amount that the owner would receive after selling a property and paying off the mortgage.

For example, fair market value: $200,000
Liens/total indebtedness = $180,000
Equity = $20,000

A is for Appreciation—an increase in value for several reasons:

- property improvement
- neighborhood improvement
- inflation
- market forces brought about by supply and demand

There is also what I call forced appreciation, which occurs when you deliberately add value to a piece of property that increases your equity position.

L is for Leverage—the use of borrowed capital to increase the potential return of an investment.

Leverage is the ability to control property with little or zero cash and increase your return on investment (ROI).

There are three kinds of leverage:

Leverage of Time—the ability to assemble your time and effectively deploy it to achieve your objective is crucial to your real estate investment. Time is a valuable resource and must be treated as such.

Leverage of People—you will be utilizing the resources of many experts to accomplish your objective. Hence, it would be best to assemble your team quickly. Experts would include mortgage brokers, attorneys, and building contractors.

Leverage of Money—without the leverage of capital, you limit your real estate investment business. One of the major limiting factors in your growth as a real estate investor is the capital needed to complete deals.

Therefore, you have to spend as much time looking for capital as you look for real estate properties.

The Cycles of Real Estate Investment

To improve your chances of getting a great deal, you should know when to buy your investment properties. Realize that prices and investment properties tend to vary seasonally. More people look to buy in summer, which tends to drive up prices.

November, December, January, and February are the ideal times to buy—so put your properties on the market during late spring and summer. Those winter months are the best time to get good bargains because that's when sellers tend to be most motivated.

Find Bargain Properties

There are external and internal factors that contribute to bargain properties.

As an investor, you will be able to find bargain properties because:

1. An anxious, motivated seller wants to unload a piece of property. Their lives may be complicated by divorce, job loss, making two payments, and things of that nature.
2. Poor physical condition of the property—abandoned properties.
3. Property in need of physical repairs—no insulation, too few bathrooms, inadequate wiring, or plumbing.

After identifying the potential properties for purchase, the investor will evaluate the properties to make sure the property fits into his criteria or his investment strategy.

Evaluating Properties

This involves developing ideas about the neighborhood and the types of property you want to invest in and own. If you want to rent in low-income areas, access to public transportation is essential. The residential quality of the neighborhood, its maintenance, is key. Is there too much traffic? Are there conveniently located parks? How about emerging communities—some investors identify these neighborhoods and start transforming the neighborhood. Investors are creative individuals!

Investment Analysis and Financial Analysis

Investment analysis is your ability to decide if a particular investment is right for your financial goals. You should specify your investment objectives and quantify them. Here are some examples:

1. My goal is to buy one investment property in the $100,000–$150,000 price range with very minimum repairs and rent it out to generate a positive monthly cash flow of $250 per month.
2. My goal is to acquire a wholesale property for $100,000 and resell it for $110,000 to an investor and gross $10,000.
3. My goal is to acquire a property for $150,000 with a fix-up cost of $50,000 (total investment, $150,000). I want to sell it to an end buyer for $200,000; my gross profit is $50,000.
4. My goal is to focus on the luxury market. I want to buy a property for $250,000 and find a hard-money lender to finance the purchase and the repairs for a total of $500,000 (rehab and other costs is $250,000). I will rehab the property with all the luxury appointments and sell the property for a gross profit

of $100,000. I will work with a front-money partner. (A front money partner is a person who has extra capital to invest in real estate projects.)

Financial Analysis

There are several ways to analyze the success of your real estate investments:

1. Detailed projection. Analyzing the potential cash-flow parameters of an investment property. Calculating a rental property's cash flow is a relatively simple process:
   - Determine the gross income from the property.
   - Deduct all expenses relating to the property.
   - Subtract any debt service relating to the property.
   - The difference is the property's cash flow.
2. Make decisions based on inspection of the property and surrounding areas.
3. Research undervalued properties in the marketplace.
4. Negotiate for a profitable deal.
5. With a buy, rehab, and sell strategy, you use the 70 percent rule. You take 70 percent of the after repair value (ARV)

Real Estate Investment and Risk

Any strategy that you select as a real estate investor has some risk attached to it. However, some techniques are riskier than others.

Risk is the chance, degree, or probability of loss in a venture or enterprise; there also is the risk that things will not come out as planned. It is in your interest to identify areas that would thwart the possible outcome that you desire. The ability to forecast a range of outcomes minimizes the risk inherent in a venture. When considering investment options, analyzing data and possible results should be a strength of a real estate investor.

Consider buying a property as a long-term rental versus buying, rehabbing, and selling. What is the relative risk associated with each strategy? Why would an investor choose to take more risk? Realize that everything being equal and taking a more significant risk means the chance for higher returns.

Here are two types of risk you may encounter:

Business risk: In a rehab project, you might need more capital than initially anticipated to complete the project.

Financial risk: This is the probability that you will be unable to make the debt service payment on the mortgage.

Basic Real Estate Investment —The Niche Investment

As an agent, you have to be knowledgeable about real estate investment because many potential clients will be asking you a lot of questions. As it stands, most agents are ill-equipped to educate and work with investors. I want to bridge that gap.

Investment focuses on three main areas:

1. Niche.

Someone once said, "There are riches in niches." A niche is a type of property the investor buys, including single-family, multi-family, apartment, mobile home, storage units, commercial, and industrial properties.

2. Strategy.

The method the investor employs to make money. This includes wholesaling, fix and flip, fix-refinance-rent, lease purchase, and a strategy called Buy, Rehab, Rent, Refinance, Repeat (popularly known as the BRRRR strategy).

3. Exit strategy.

How do investors intend to remove themselves from the deal? Are you holding the property long-term and renting? Are you flipping for quick cash? Are you refinancing, taking cash, and renting?

7

Principles of an Exit Strategy

Having a specific exit strategy is crucial to success as the correct approach will result in maximized profits. It's never wise to enter a real estate investing deal without having a clear understanding of how you will profit from the deal.

These are some exit strategies available to the real estate investor:

1. Rent. This is the conventional way to generate income from your investment properties. It does not involve ownership as far as the tenant is concerned, and you, as owner and landlord, are responsible for maintaining the property.
2. Rent-to-own. You commit to renting a property for a specific time, giving tenants the option to buy the property before their lease runs out. In some cases, a percentage of the rent is applied to the purchase price. The arrangement, most times, encourages the tenant to plan for ownership soon.
3. Lease purchase. An agreement between a buyer and seller to purchase a property within a specified time. A portion of the lease payment is credited to the buyer as a down payment. Those payments may enable the buyer to purchase the property outright.

Such a tenant/buyer has a specific time to buy the property.

4. Sandwich lease. You lease a property from an owner and then sublease to tenants. The money you make comes from the difference between what you pay the owner of the property and the total amount of money you receive from the tenants. The mastery and application of this technique could make you a lot of money.

5. Lease option. A technique of gaining control of a property, not ownership—but the right to possess a property now and purchase that property later with terms you define today. Lease options are tremendous tools available to real estate investors, and with the understanding of this concept, you can control millions of dollars in real estate.

6. A purchase option. The optionor (seller) agrees to give the optionee (buyer) the exclusive right to purchase the leased property. The tenant/buyer can exercise his option to buy during the option, which usually corresponds with the lease period.

NOTE: An option is not the same as a standard purchase contract, a bilateral agreement. A bilateral contract legally binds both parties to the agreement, whereas an option binds only the seller. An optionee is not obligated to buy; he simply has that option.

7. "Subject to." Obtaining the deed to a property without acquiring a new loan or mortgage. Rather, the seller signs over the deed to his property "subject to" the existing mortgage. The buyer makes the mortgage payment, but does not secure a mortgage to acquire the property.

You can use a "subject to" technique to acquire or sell a piece of property. For example, assume a seller owes $195,000 on a home that is worth $195,000. Because he has no equity, he might very well be willing to give you the deed to the property.

Sometimes a seller might even pay you to take over the deed. If the buyer sells in the conventional way, he might need to pay a real estate commission. If the seller pays $3,000 for an investor to take over the mortgage, he might be better off.

In the early 2000s, when I was an active investor, I completed several "subject to" deals whereby owners paid my investors to take over their properties. The investors acquired the properties, cleaned and fixed them, and resold them for profit. To buy these properties, we put up numerous "bandit signs" that contain such inscriptions as "We Buy Your Property for Cash." We got many calls from property owners who were behind on their mortgages or faced foreclosure.

"Subject to" means you can:

- Have the title in your name—full ownership.
- Seller might pay you to take over the payment.
- Easier to prove "seasoning of title"* when you are the title holder.
- Easier to refinance because of "seasoning."
- If you are on the title, you will have long-term gains rather than short-term profits if you hold the home for longer than twelve months.

8. Contract for deed (also called an installment contract). A buyer makes an installment payment on a piece of property, similar to how automobile financing works. In this transaction, the seller holds legal title to the property as security or collateral for payment, while the buyer has an "equitable" title. When the

---

* "Seasoning of title" usually refers to the length of time that a homeowner has owned a particular home.

buyer pays the total amount due under the contract, the seller delivers the legal title to the buyer.

An equitable title gives the buyer the right to live in the property, improve it, rent it, and otherwise enjoy all of the benefits of ownership. However, because buyers do not have a legal title, they cannot use the property as collateral for a home equity loan.

However, because the IRS treats a contract for deed as a sale, the buyer has tax benefits of ownership. A contract-for-deed seller must report the transaction as an installment sale on IRS Form 6252. Once sold, the seller cannot claim depreciation or any other tax benefits of the property. If the buyer defaults, the seller can foreclose.

9. Wraparound mortgage (also called an inclusive trust deed or mortgage). A device used whenever there is a low interest, assumable loan against the property, and some equity exceeding the original loan amount.

For example, rather than pass the old interest loan onto the buyer, the seller can decide to earn some interest on the lender's money. The seller offers to carry the first loan or mortgage for the buyer. The seller can charge an interest rate between the interest rate on the old loan and the market rate for new loans while making payments on the old loan and keeping the difference.

Here's an illustration:

A $100,000 property has a $60,000 loan at 7 percent with a monthly payment at $339.19. A buyer agrees to buy the property for $100,000, with the seller carrying the entire loan amount at 10 percent interest, which comes with monthly payments of $877.50. The seller accordingly pockets $478 a month for the next thirty years. (Note that the seller earns 10 percent a year interest on his $40,000 equity and 3 percent a year interest on the lender's $60,000.) The benefit for the buyer is that he is acquiring this property with zero cash. The seller of the property is secured because the property is security for the wraparound mortgage.

NOTE: This method makes the seller feel secure, especially sellers who are leery of carrying a second mortgage.

Illustration:

Value of property	$100,000 @ 10%
1st Mortgage	$60,000 @ 7%
Equity	$40,000 @ 3%

Seller agrees to "wrap" his old loan of $60,000 at 7 percent around the $100,000—the value of the property—at 10 percent with a monthly payment of $877.50.

The difference to the seller is $877.50 - $399.19 = $478

When there is no equity in a deal, the owner can also use a wraparound mortgage to make money

Here is an illustration:

Property Value	$100,000
Property Price	$100,000
Seller sells property at 10 percent interest	$877.57
Seller old loan at 5 percent interest	$536.82
The difference to the SELLER is	$340.00

Understanding these types of creative financing will make you a lot of money.

NOTE: These exit strategies like "Subject to," Contract for deed, Wraparound mortgage, create a borrower— lender relationships—which means borrower enjoys all the tax benefits associated with home ownership, while the lender has the right to foreclose in case the borrower defaults in the payment of the mortgage obligations.

8

Understanding Wholesale Investment Strategy

T he flipper investor buys or controls properties at or below wholesale prices and resells property at a profit to other investors or the retail market. Here are four types of flipper investors:

1. The Finder (bird dog). Gathers information on potential properties and sells the information to other investors. You can start as a finder, or bird dog, because it does not take any cash or prior knowledge to look for distressed properties that could be fixed up. The finder gathers the information and sells it to other investors for a fee. The finder can command a fee of $500 to $1,000 per transaction.

2. The Wholesaler. Finds a bargain property and signs a purchase contract. He can close on the property and sell it outright or sell his contract to other investors. Many individuals and companies wholesale properties. "We Buy Ugly Properties" is one of the biggest wholesalers in the country. I know a wholesaler who has been able to develop the wholesaling business to a science. He acquires the properties, draws the sketch of the

property, gives the investor repair estimates, submits comparables (comps) from appraisals, and gives you all the vital investment numbers that the investor needs to make a buying decision. No wonder his properties stay on the market for less than a week—they are hot commodities. Most wholesalers use PropStream* (www.propstream.com) to find vacant, tax delinquent, and foreclosed properties.

3. The Rehabber: Someone who buys wholesale properties to fix them to sell to an owner-occupant buyer or a retail investor. The retail investor buys the property intending to rent it out or make a lease purchase. The exit strategy chosen by the rehabber would depend on how he fixes the property. If the rehabber wants to command top dollar, he will bring the property up to "doll house" condition with all the sizzling features.

4. The Retailer: Usually someone who buys a property that needs minor repair work. He will do the cosmetic repairs, such as painting or installing carpeting, then rent out or do a lease purchase.

Wholesaling Properties for Quick Profit

The business of finding distressed properties and quickly selling the deals for a quick cash profit.

The goal in real estate wholesaling is to sell the home to an interested party before the contract with the original homeowner closes. This means no money changes hands between the wholesaler and the seller, not at least until a buyer is found by the wholesaler. The wholesaler makes a profit by finding a buyer willing to purchase the home at a price higher than the amount agreed upon by the buyer. The difference in price—paid for by the buyer—is the profit, retained by the wholesaler.

---

* PropStream is a comprehensive online platform for real estate investors.

Example of Real Estate Wholesaling

Real estate wholesaling may sound complicated. But it's really very simple. Here's an example:

Let's say an owner decides to sell his property, which is very run down and needs a lot of work. A wholesaler offers to pay cash for the property, which the owner lacks the resources to fix up. The owner and the wholesaler agree to put the house under contract for $110,000. The wholesaler, using his network of investors, finds an eager buyer at $120,000. He assigns the contract to this investor, who then has a profitable fixer-upper project. The wholesaler makes a $10,000 profit without ever owning the home.

From this example, we see that there was never actually an offer to purchase from the wholesaler. He agreed to contract the house out for the homeowner to an interested party. Under the contract, the buyer pays $120,000 to the wholesaler, who pays the homeowner $110,000, keeping the rest for himself as profit.

The Four Components of a Wholesaling

1. Cash buyers (investors and rehabbers)
2. Motivated sellers: those who are motivated to buy for multiple reasons
3. Creative solutions to real estate investment
4. Marketing system/communication systems: the wholesale investor has a network of cash buyers

Making the Wholesale Process Work

a) Find cash buyers in advance, if possible.
b) Find a good deal by seeking motivated sellers. These are often people in the middle of a divorce, relocating for a new job, or struggling to pay taxes or the mortgage. (www.propstream.com is a great resource.)
c) Analyze the deal: do the numbers make sense?
d) Tie up the deal under a "buying contract" or buy the property.
e) Wholesalers contact investor or ask buyers about the deal.

f) Pass the deal along for a referral fee via assignment of contract or simultaneous closing.

g) Close the deal, get paid, and go to the bank.

The Mechanics of a Wholesale Deal

- The low-end market: typically provides your greatest volume of deals.
- The mid-class market: prices may be high to resell (mostly in subdivisions—prices tend to be the same).
- The upper-end market should be avoided for wholesale flips because they contain mostly very high mortgage payments for investors. These work best for skilled investors who can raise money from other passive investors.

Deals Investors Should Avoid

1. Ones with meager margins
2. Very depressed areas
3. No legitimate out in your contract (it always should have an escape clause)

Crunching the Numbers for a Classic Wholesale Deal

After Repair Value ARV = $200,000
Multiply by 70% (the 70 percent rule)*
$140,000
$40,000 is the rehab cost
$140,000–$40,000
Subtract rehab costs = $40,000

---

* The 70 percent rule states that an investor should pay no more than 70 percent of the after repair value (ARV) of a property minus the repairs needed. The ARV is what a home is worth after it is fully repaired.

Final wholesale price = $100,000—the cash investor will pay this price for the house.

In this scenario, the wholesaler should be able to pick up the property for $90,000 to sell it to the cash investor for $100,000.

9

Financing the Deal

Investment property loans are designed for an investor to maximize their returns by leveraging the down payment, the length of the payback terms, and the interest rate. Investors can further improve their returns by using investment loans to build where there is a need for affordable houses to rent, for instance, or to rehab a property to increase its value and cash flow.

However, investment properties are considered higher risk than residential loans for a personal residence. The logic behind this is that if something goes wrong and the property loses money for the investor, it's easier to walk away from a property if it's not your residence.

Here are various investment loans that the investor can consider and explore:

1. Conventional Residential Mortgages

These are loans obtained from traditional lenders, such as large banks or credit unions. Typically, these loans require a minimum 20 percent down payment.

Conventional mortgages are used to finance single-family homes, duplexes, triplexes, and quadplexes—but loans on properties with more than four units fall in the "commercial" category, which we'll cover in a bit.

Restrictions imposed by federal housing agencies Fannie Mae and Freddie Mac usually limit investors to carrying four conventional mortgages, though this number can climb to ten depending on the bank and the position of the borrower.

For most active investors, techniques other than conventional mortgages comprise the bulk of their investments. Therefore, understanding other creative financing techniques is imperative for an investor-friendly agent.

2. Federal Housing Administration Loans

FHA loans can be used for multifamily investment properties of up to four units, provided the investor lives in one of the units.

Investors may not carry more than one FHA loan at a time, so this is not a strategy for most active investors.

A subset of the FHA loan, the 203K loan, allows homeowners to wrap needed home remodeling into the cost of the property. This can also be used for small multifamily properties when the owner lives in one of the units. Although the red tape involved can be a little cumbersome, the 203K loan can be an awesome tool to help new investors build immediate sweat equity into their properties.

3. Portfolio Loans

A type of mortgage that a lender originates and retains instead of offloading on the secondary mortgage market. Because a portfolio loan is kept in the lender's portfolio, or "on the books," the lender sets the standards, sometimes favorably for borrowers. Portfolio loans are not sold to Fannie Mae or Freddie Mac, and they come with strict standards—therefore, they can be more flexible. Many small community banks offer portfolio loans and are able to customize a loan program for homeowners or investors. To find a lender who specializes in portfolio loans, an investor simply needs to pick up the phone—most portfolio lenders are not shy to tout their loan programs.

4. Commercial Loans

These loans are designed for commercial properties or residential properties of more than four units. A typical commercial loan will usually be amortized for a maximum of twenty-five years but with a balloon payment due after five.

5. Hard Money

A way to borrow without using traditional mortgage lenders. Loans come from individuals or investors who front the money based on the property you're using as collateral.

Such loans carry an interest rate between 10 and 15 percent, depending on the lender. However, because the term length is typically less than a year, the high interest rate doesn't actually affect the deal that significantly—unless the property doesn't sell quickly.

Additionally, hard money lenders generally charge fees known as "points" (a point is 1 percent of the loan amount), which are sometimes paid upfront and occasionally wrapped into the loan.

Here is a statement from a typical hard money lender—loan closed in 2020:

> After Repair Value – ARV - $600,000
> Collateral: First lien, assignment of leases/rents, fixtures, and personal guaranty
> Strategy: $356,000
> Interest Rate: 13%
> Loan to Value (LTV): 59.3%
> LTC: 89.9%
> Borrower: 50 Warren St LLC
> Approval Signature: Date Agreed:
> LOAN SUMMARY Payable To:
> Application Hard Money Lender - POC $495.00
> Underwriting/Processing Hard Money Lender, LLC $500.00

Broker Fee 1.0% $3,560.00
Origination Hard Money Lender, LLC 2.0% $7,120.00
Feasibility & Appraisal POC $ -
Prepaid Inspections - @ $150 -
Prepaid Interest 86 Days $11,056.16
$128.56 Per Diem
Attorney/Title Charges (estimated) Purchase $2,295.00
Transfer Fees $249.90
Tax Proration (estimated) Annual Taxes $3,852.00
($1,979.50)
Past Due Taxes/Utilities: (if applicable) $ -
Purchase Price/Payoff $249,900.00
Construction Holdback $146,000.00
Total Costs $419,196.56
LESS: Loan Amount $ (356,000.00)
ESTIMATED Cash From/(Due) Borrower at or Prior
to Closing - EM not incl: $63,196.56

Example:

An investor is looking to flip a house but he's short on funds. So, he finds a hard money lender who agrees to fund the cost of acquisition and the repairs. The ARV is $600,000, and the hard money lender charges 12 percent interest with three points wrapped into the loan. The cost of repairs is $146,000. An investor would pay $275,000 to rehab and flip the house.
Using the 70 percent rule: $600,000 X 0.70%
Investor would offer $420,000 - $146,000 = $274,000
Investor will offer $274,000 for the property

6. Private Money

Similar to hard money in many respects, private money is usually distinguishable by the relationship between the lender and the borrower. The lender is not professional but rather an individual looking to achieve higher returns on their cash. Often, there is a closer relationship between the lender and the borrower (such as a family member, friend, or coworker). Such lenders are often much less business-oriented than hard money lenders. Private money usually has fewer fees and points, and term length can be negotiated more easily to serve the best interest of both parties. Private lenders will lend you cash to buy property in exchange for a specific interest rate. Their investment is secured by a promissory note or mortgage on the property, which means if you don't pay, the lender can foreclose and take the house (just like a bank, hard money, or most other loan types). The interest rate given to a private lender is usually established up front, and loan terms can range from six months to thirty years.

7. Front Money Partners

Simply, individuals who have money available to participate in real estate deals, front money partners can be either debt or equity partners.

Both can help you raise all the money you need to fund your real estate deals, but they work quite differently.

Debt partners will lend you money for your deals in exchange for a specific interest rate. Their investment is secured by a promissory note or mortgage on the property and property insurance. The interest rate they charge is usually established up front, and the money is loaned for a specific period.

Primarily, debt partners are used in deals that one investor can finance. They are also commonly used when you believe you can raise the value of the property quickly. You can take on a debt partner in that situation, and once you add the value to the investment, refinance it and pay back the partner. The deal needs to have enough income to cover the interest payments to the private money partner to take them on. You also have to be sure that you can cover paying off the loan when it is due.

Equity partners, meanwhile, invest money into your property in exchange for an ownership percentage. This allows them to participate in all aspects of property ownership. They typically receive a return on their investment under their ownership percentage that includes cash flow, appreciation, loan paydown, and any depreciation.

On the other hand, equity partners will invest money into your property in exchange for an ownership percentage. The ownership of the property allows them to participate in all aspects of the property.

Front money participation will help you structure the deal as you see fit to your overall strategy in your capital structure.

8. Equity Partnerships

If your investor client can't finance a property on their own, a good solution can also be to use a partner who can make the deal happen. This can be structured in several ways:

- Both partners split funding and pay cash.
- One partner supplies all the funding, purchases the property with cash; the other manages the property, makes repairs.
- One partner supplies the down payment; the other secures the mortgage.
- Both partners supply the down payment, but one partner gets the mortgage.

There are numerous ways to structure a deal like this but be sure to advise your client to seek legal assistance when setting up the structure for the partnership. Partnerships can be an excellent tool for investors, but only when done properly.

The Evolution of Hard Money

Ask most people how long they believe the credit system has been around, and you'll find that the majority think of it as a relatively recent invention. Believe it or not, the concept of hard money is considered to be one the earliest forms of credit financing, dating back to the eighteenth century.

Historians believe that Hammurabi, the ruler of Babylon, invented one of the first lending systems. Many other civilizations, such as the Roman Empire, Tang Dynasty, and Spanish Empire, developed their own hard money loans.

These days, hard money loans are most common in the US and Canada. The term "hard money" is used almost exclusively to describe a short-term loan from private lenders. Hard money has remained unregulated by state and federal law outside of being subject to a few interest rate restrictions. These are often considered loans of last resort or short-term bridge loans. Here is how they work:

The funds come from an individual or company, not a bank, and are used primarily for real estate transactions.

Typically taken out for a short time, a hard money loan is a great way to raise money quickly, but comes at a higher cost and lower loan to value.

Hard money loan terms generally can be negotiated between the lender and the borrower and typically use the property as collateral.

The modern banking system offers a wide variety of credit options—from mortgages to credit cards, but hard money loans have long been vital to the real estate sector.

During the Great Depression, the collapse of the banking industry resulted in individuals pulling their money out of bank accounts and keeping it at home, which ultimately led to a mass reduction in the amount of money in circulation. Lenders tried to resolve this crisis by offering loans that utilized real estate as collateral. Due to the risky nature of this type of loan, higher interest rates were charged, but with no other way to get quick cash, many property owners had no alternatives other than to take out this form of hard money loans.

Since then, hard money's vitality ebbed and flowed. In the 1950s, for example, private short-term debt was essential to the world of real estate development.

By the early 1990s, a significant turn in the commercial real estate market resulted in an unprecedented number of banks failing or experiencing massive losses. Accordingly, private lenders became a widely popular alternative when it came to real estate financing.

During the early 2000s, a lack of regulation and an increase in speculation created a real estate bubble that crashed with a vengeance. Foreclosures spiked by more than 225 percent between 2006 and 2008, with foreclosure filings hitting a record-breaking 3.1 million in 2008 alone.

Hard money loans have unfairly developed an unsavory reputation for being predatory, mainly because they've been misunderstood or misused. However, if appropriately used, hard money loans serve a valuable purpose for investors and borrowers, both in good times and in times of national financial crisis.

According to research, private lending had more than doubled by the 2010s, and private debt within the US grew to more than a whopping $700 billion.

So, why did private lending suddenly develop a better reputation in such a short span? It was mainly due to real estate investors becoming increasingly frustrated with the Dodd-Frank Act, aimed at regulating the banking industry but requiring them to jump through numerous hoops. Investors began looking for alternative lending solutions and quickly realized that the once-called "back-alley operators" were now a viable, respectable alternative. Private lenders developed a new reputation of being established, above-board providers of smart lending solutions with billions in Assets Under Management (AUM). Assets under management (AUM) is the total market value of the investments that a person or entity manages on behalf of clients. Assets under management definitions and formulas vary by company. In the calculation of AUM, some financial institutions include bank deposits, mutual funds, and cash in their calculation.

Investors have discovered that private lending offers a variety of perks that traditional banks cannot provide, such as better speed and execution of loans, unique loan terms that include rehab costs, and the ability to provide more leverage.

Lending has changed considerably in the past decade. Hard money interest rates averaged 18 percent between 2009 and 2012 when very little capital was available in private borrowing due to the real estate market being at its lowest.

With institutional lending being stifled, real estate investors had no choice but to rely on private lenders for hard money loans. As a result, private lenders leveraged this opportunity to fill a void left behind by Wall Street. Ultimately, this helped private lenders prove that their approach can be scalable and has earned its place in the world of real estate investment lending.

As today's real estate market improves, interest rates on private loans have dropped as low as 7 percent.

In the 2010s, the Federal Reserve made interest rate cuts that allowed private lenders to acquire lower-cost capital, thus allowing them to pass that on to real estate investors by offering them better terms.

Homogenization has also driven the reduction of rates and fees, with private lenders entering the arena of real estate lending at startling rates.

Following the housing crisis, we've also watched house flipping go mainstream. With television shows like *Property Brothers* becoming incredibly popular among the masses, it has spawned a new generation of fix-and-flip enthusiasts. This, of course, has led to a need for even more capital and financing options.

Gone are the days of Wall Street snubbing hard money lenders. Having witnessed the success of many investors, Wall Street has noticed what hard money lenders are doing right and now want a piece of the action.

With many more banks entering the arena of fix-and-flip loans by offering lines of credit to lenders, the cost of funding loans has dropped.

As Wall Street has become more involved in private lending, it also has led to securitization, which provides legitimacy to the industry and shows acceptance in the eyes of investment bankers.

Private lending has come a long way and has finally earned a reputation for being a trustworthy, legitimate provider of hard money real estate loans. The industry will continue its upward trajectory of growth if we can continue providing reasonable rates and terms.

Let's not forget that we've enjoyed a prosperous time in the housing market for almost a decade. It is important to remember that you need to be prepared for rainy days to remain successful in hard money lending and real estate investing. Make sure you have a solid long-term game plan should those rainy days arrive.

Following the great housing crisis of 2008, we witnessed the staying power of hard money and its ability to fill a gap that ultimately helped the housing market rebound. With that in mind, we feel confident that the future of hard money lending is bright.

We're living in an exciting time in which the hard money industry is finally earning the respect it has long deserved. It's found its place in the mainstream and will only continue to grow and maintain its newfound positive reputation.

Summary on Financing

These eight financing strategies I've outlined above are some of the most common but are definitely not the entire list. Creative financing is a field that investors explore, learn, and grow their knowledge of throughout their careers. You, as an agent, do not need to understand the entire process, but by having a general idea of the different financing options available, you become a more valuable asset to an investor's team. This hopefully allows you to close more transactions and grow your business. This does not preclude you from employing some of these techniques yourself.

10

Borrow Your Way to
Real Estate Riches

O ne of the limiting factors in completing a transaction is borrowing the capital. Therefore, it behooves the investor to
find creative ways to fund a transaction. Here are several ways to
borrow money:

1. Signature loan. A loan based, basically, on your
   signature and a promise to repay your lender. In this
   case, the loan is given based on good credit history.
   No collateral is needed in this type of loan.
2. Collateral loan. You offer something of value to the
   lender as security for the loan. For example, you
   might offer your home, automobile, jewels, stocks,
   bonds, or boat. Remember that lenders are always
   willing to loan money when they know that the loan
   will be repaid. If you lack collateral, you can borrow
   from a friend, a business partner, or you can rent
   from a "collateral entrepreneur," i.e., somebody
   who does this as a regular business. It is easier to
   borrow from a lender when you have collateral. The
   lender knows your collateral protects its investment.
3. Cosigned loan. This might be considered "a living

collateral" by the lender. A suitable cosigner should possess the following qualifications:

    a. Steady job or profitable business

    b. Good credit history

    c. Telephone, bank account, and a few credit cards

Your application becomes stronger when you use a cosigner. To encourage somebody to cosign a loan, you might wish to consider paying the cosigner a fee for signing your loan application and promissory note. Even a small fee might change somebody's mind quickly.

4. Note as Collateral. The note carried by a seller of real estate or business could be used to finance any real estate deal. Any form of debt owed to you can be used as collateral to finance a real estate deal. This process also can be called paper collateral or note. Paper collateral is any kind of financial document that pays you an income and has a transactional value.

    a. Examples of paper collateral:

    b. Promissory note from other people to you

    c. Account receivable

    d. Stocks, bonds, certificates of deposit, savings accounts, mutual funds, investments, etc.

    e. Leases

    f. Income from contracts

5. Through relatives, friends, and business partners. However, to avoid misunderstandings, I suggest that a simple contract be written to repay such loans. All terms should be spelled out in the contract.

Friends and business partners are very good sources to acquire funds for your deals—but just do it the right way.

Creative Financing

In its simplest form, creative financing is essentially any alternative means of financing a real estate deal that doesn't involve an institutionalized lender. As its name suggests, creative financing draws from sources that the general census is typically unaware of—hence the "creative" designation. It is worth noting that creative financing includes numerous sources.

In real estate investing there are two ways to structure a deal with sellers of properties:

1. Using cash or obtaining traditional financing, which is what the bulk of buyers employ.
2. Using creative financing techniques, which are alternative ways of buying property without any kind of traditional financing or cash deal.

As an investor and agent, the more familiar you are with creative real estate financing, the more deals you will complete, and the more money you will make. Creative real estate financing has advantages for both the seller and the buyer. Sellers earn more money in terms of the price of the property and the interest rate; buyers can acquire the property with very little or no money down and can accomplish more deals.

Seller Financing. An unconventional creative financing method is "seller financing" or "owner financing." Sometimes we call it "owner carry back." With seller financing, the seller will agree to sell the property to the buyer with little or no money and then owner-finance or carry the balance owned in the form of a seller-finance loan. What this means is that the seller becomes the lender or the bank so to speak.

Example: You buy a property from Seller Jones for $100,000. Rather than borrow the mortgage money from the bank, Seller Jones agrees to finance or carry back 95 percent of the amount—$95,000. So, with just $5,000 that the buyer borrowed from an uncle, you can acquire the property without using your own money.

In such an instance, ownership transfers to the buyer, and the seller becomes the lender. The seller is protected with a mortgage lien on the property and would collect the mortgage payment, including interest.

Land Contract. You can also use this type of contract if you are in a mortgage state* or a "contract for deed" if you are in a trust deed state.† At the closing, you sign two documents: the promissory note and the deed that transfers the mortgage to the owner.

A land contract is similar to seller financing, except that you don't get legal title to the property until after you meet the terms of the contract. In a land contract, you, the buyer or investor, have an "equitable title" in the property. You have an interest in the property, but you do not have the actual title. With a land contract, the buyer can protect his equitable interest by filing a "memorandum of land contract." This puts the public on notice of the buyer or investor's interest in the property. If the seller tries to sell, the memorandum will cloud the title and will prevent the sale.

Land contracts, if structured properly, benefit both the buyer and the seller. As an investor, a land contract allows you to buy a property with little or no money down.

"Subject to" Financing. This term describes acquiring a property with an existing mortgage, but the buyer does not become personally liable for the mortgage repayment

However, the buyer must make mortgage payments to keep

---

* Mortgage State: In mortgage states, the mortgage is, technically, not the loan a homebuyer takes out but a document that gives the lender a lien on the property, states money instructor. In some states, the lender retains title until the mortgage is paid off, while in others, the borrower holds the title. In any mortgage state, the lender may begin foreclosure to take over the property if the borrower defaults on his loan.

† Trust Deed State: In the deed of trust states, instead of a mortgage, lenders use a trust deed to assign a third party—the trustee—to hold title until the debt is paid off. Some states allow attorneys to serve as trustees; in others, such as California, mortgage loan brokers can be trustees.

the property from going into foreclosure. In the event of a default, the only part of the property that is lost is the buyer's equity.

In acquiring a subject to deal, most investors create a contract that transfers the deed to them but not the liability. This allows the investor to control the property and rent it or sell it and acquire an appreciation that might occur. The original mortgage is paid when the investor sells the property.

When you transfer the deed, it might trigger a clause in the loan called "due on sale" where the lender could call the loan due, but the reality is that as far as the loan is being paid, the original lender might know that you have engineered a "subject to" deal. It is advisable to have an attorney write the contract.

Illustration and a Case Study:

An investor finds a motivated seller (his house faces foreclosure because he has lost his job). The mortgage on the property is $160,500, but the house has a value of $245,500. The monthly payment is $1,050 in principle, interest, taxes, and insurance (PITI). The investor pays $6,700 in back payments, including closing costs to work out the deal with the seller. The investor also pays the owner another $9,500 for out-of-pocket costs of $16,200.

After the investor closed on the deal with the owner, he sold the property to a buyer for $249,000. At closing, the investor paid off the existing loan of $160,500 and $16,200 of personal expenses. After making a monthly payment of $1050, the investor walked away with $67,500 in profit.

Lease Options. Creative lease options allow an investor to take over a piece of property with very little down. Lease options give the investor other avenues to explore what to do with the property while you have control of it. Lease-option contracts give the investor/buyer the right to buy the home at a specific time.

A lease-purchase contract requires you to buy it. It is important to know that the option part of the agreement means that the investor/buyer has the option to buy but he is not obligated to buy.

Conversely, the seller is obligated. Put simply, lease options bind the seller to sell, but do not bind the buyer to purchase.

11

Making Offers for the Investor

You have to learn to be comfortable making offers on behalf of investors. An investor will make an offer based on the analysis. The current crop of investors you will be working with value speed and accuracy. Most of the people you will be working with would like you to do your due diligence before making offers.

For instance, I will meet with my investors to devise a strategy for making our offers. Generally, most of them are paying cash and can close in ten to fourteen days if the title has cleared. If my investor is working with a hard money lender, I know we can close in less than twenty-one days. I also know in advance if they are buying, fixing and selling, or buying to rent. As an agent working with an investor, I don't go around low-balling offers.

Most wholesalers already have done such analyses, so making an offer for a rehab investor is even easier. You merely need to verify that the wholesaler's analysis study makes investment sense, and the numbers are correct.

Having worked with many investors, I believe they want to acquire property, make money with it, and build wealth. They will make the offer and acquire the property if the numbers make sense.

Their formula in acquiring the property is simple—investors typically offer cash to close in fourteen days, with three days' inspection. However, it could be twenty-one days to close when using hard money lenders, with seven days due diligence and the probability that the lender will do an appraisal.

Remember, with today's technology, e-sign, and other formats, submitting offers on behalf of investors has become easier and faster. Investors have been through numerous deals, so they do not need tutoring to sign the offers. They are motivated to do a deal.

Suppose you, as an agent, have acquired the real estate investment knowledge and know the strategy the investor is applying to buy his property. In that case, it should be a joy to work with an investor because you know what he is trying to accomplish; your role is to help facilitate the transaction to a smooth closing.

Remember that an experienced investor is not simply throwing out wild numbers to see what might happen. Most seasoned investors have done their math and determined a price that makes sense and know from experience how many of their offers might be accepted.

Illustration

A wholesaler sends me a deal for one of my investors. The wholesale price was $134,900. New construction in the area was going for about $600,000. So, this deal was a no-brainer. The property was a teardown, and the new construction budget will be about $250,000. Teardown and pre-construction, including purchase of the property, will come to about $160,000.

Price and preconstruction cost	= $160,000
Construction cost plus	= $250,000
Total Cost	= $400,000
Comps or After Repair Value	= $600,000
Gross Profit	= $200,000

There is no need to haggle or negotiate the price—the investor knew the strategy going into the deal and the profit potential involved, so we offered full asking price. The property was an off-market property that was being sold by a wholesaler. As an investor/agent, I get such wholesale deals all the time that I share with my investors.

12

Selling a Property for the Investor

I believe it's important to state an obvious truth: don't exaggerate the after repair value (ARV). So, it's crucial to make sure the after repair value (ARV) is solid and validated. You don't want a situation in which the property is appraised for less than the ARV.

In other words, when dealing with investors, be careful to give them a reasonable selling price; don't pad the price just so the investor will work with you. Working with an investor can be a career-changing move because of the multiple deals you'll get. However, if you exaggerate prices, you may display your inability to sell the property should they choose to use you. Then, you've lost that client forever.

For an investor, it often comes down to one important word: speed.

This is especially true for flippers, as the holding costs can quickly eat up any profits in the property. When selling an owner-occupied property, the family generally balances "price" more than "speed." Not so for investors. Obviously, the price matters and getting the highest price possible is great. However, a home sitting on the market for six months because it is priced too high can be financially devastating for an investor who is making an exorbitant interest payment and other related holding costs, such as landscaping, utility payments, and maintenance. Such items add up quickly.

Everyone has an opinion of how much their property is worth. You may believe that a property is worth only $150,000 when the investor believes it can achieve $200,000. This is why I believe it's essential that an agent be involved from the beginning, helping the investor determine the ARV during the initial purchase phase.

Eleven Ways to Find Real Estate Investors

1. Real estate investment clubs: Groups of investors meet regularly to learn, network, and make deals. I have always maintained that real estate investment is like an underground economy where plenty of deals are being made, but unless you are involved, you will never know. Seek to provide value at these meetings, maybe offer to speak. Show your expertise, and you'll attract attention.

2. Establish yourself as an expert in real estate investment: You can write a blog about real estate investing and discuss emerging neighborhoods to invest in, investment strategies, and interview investors.

3. Be a resource for real estate investors: Use social media to showcase your expertise in real estate investment. There are several real estate groups on Facebook that you can join to showcase your knowledge and meet other investors.

4. Organize a seminar on real estate investment: As a former real estate investment instructor, I gained many investors through my teaching as I became an expert on real estate investment and wrote many e-books on real estate investment.

5. BiggerPockets: This is an online real estate investing site where investors congregate. It is effortless to search by area and connect with local investors.

6. Local REIA meetings: Almost every city has a local real estate investors association meeting. These are

held on a weekly or monthly basis. For the value you receive, the membership fees are very low. It's a great place to meet both new and experienced investors.

7. Meetup.com: Many investors host weekly or monthly meetings. They are a great way to learn about investing and connect with some active and high-profile clients.

8. Facebook: In my area, I belong to several Facebook groups, many of which have hundreds of investors. We all exchange deals or ask questions. It's a great spot to be an agent because you can forge relationships and see deals that might interest your buyers.

9. Multiple Listing Service (MLS): If you see a nicely remodeled house hit the market, find out who the seller is. See what else they have done. Send them a personal letter saying you'd like to meet for coffee to discuss how you can help them find more deals.

10. REI-USA: A very active real estate online community that has various subject experts.

11. Agents in your office: Let them know that you work with real estate investors. My experience has been that many agents do not want to mess with investors. Most agents don't want to or even try to work with investors or the investment world.

If you know some investor/buyers and can understand even a little about the investment basics, you can be the go-to agent in your office for either off-market or soon-to-be listings. Your investor clients love these types of deals and can also close quickly on them.

All you have to do is get one or two quality investor/buyers and then mention to other agents that if they come across any rehab properties, to please tell you first.

Think about it this way: Have you ever heard an agent tell you about a listing appointment in which the house was so dirty or unkempt they declined the listing? Or perhaps an agent refused to list a house because the commission was too small? Or dreaded taking a listing of a property in need of repairs that the owner can't or won't make?

You should be involved in such scenarios. If you have the quality investor/buyer, you can easily put together a quick deal that works for everyone.

13

Understanding Foreclosure Investing

There are numerous riches and opportunities in the foreclosure market. Knowing how to identify the opportunities is key for an investor.

But because of its complexity, many investors shy away from investing in foreclosure.

Each state has laws that govern the foreclosure process, including the notices a lender must post publicly, the homeowner's options for bringing the loan current and avoiding foreclosure, and the timeline and process for selling the property.

A foreclosure—as in the actual act of a lender seizing a property—is typically the final step after a lengthy pre-foreclosure process. Before foreclosure, the lender may offer several alternatives to avoid foreclosure, many of which can mediate a foreclosure's negative consequences for both the buyer and the seller.

In twenty-two states—including Florida, Illinois, and New York—judicial foreclosure is the norm. This is where the lender must go through the courts to get permission to foreclose by proving the borrower is delinquent. If the foreclosure is approved, the local sheriff auctions the property to the highest bidder to recoup what the bank is owed. The bank then becomes the owner and sells the property through the traditional route to recoup its losses.

I live in Georgia, so I am familiar with its market for foreclosures. Georgia is a "non-judicial foreclosure" state. That means the lender can foreclose on your home without filing a lawsuit or appearing in court. The procedures for foreclosure are spelled out in the Official Code of Georgia, Sections 44-14-162 through 44-14-162.4.

Other states might have a different foreclosure process, so you, as an investor, have to be familiar with your state's foreclosure procedures.

When you buy property, you borrow the money from a lender and sign two documents: the note (or promissory note) and the security deed. The note spells out the terms of the payment agreement. The security deed is the instrument that conveys title to the lender until the debt is paid in full. After the debt is paid off, the lender marks the note paid and the security deed "satisfied," and the title reverts to the borrower.

The foreclosure process sets in when the borrower defaults in paying his mortgage obligation.

Three Primary Ways to Buy Foreclosed Properties

1. The Pre-Foreclosure Stage: Occurs when the borrower defaults and might want to sell the property before it winds up in court at the auction stage. The pre-foreclosure stage presents a lot of opportunities for the savvy investor. You can use creative real estate financing methods to acquire some of these pre-foreclosure properties. Remember, too, that short sales occur during this stage. You can be a paid subscriber to a service that supplies pre-foreclosure leads.

Once the foreclosure process starts, the borrower becomes a "distressed seller" because the property is in jeopardy, and the distressed seller is eager to sell at any price. Therein also lies the hidden fortune in foreclosure. Most properties go into foreclosure because of personal rather than physical reasons. The main reason is that some calamity occurred, and the owner could not afford the house. Some of the problems include job loss, relocation, divorce, family problems, business failures, financial crises, IRS/tax problems, out-of-state owners. All these can cause an owner to fall behind on their mortgage obligations.

Investors can buy the property during the pre-foreclosure stage. There are many strategies, including bringing the mortgage obligation current and taking over the original payment. Remember that in the pre-foreclosure stage the seller is:

- Very motivated to sell and you, the investor/buyer, can leverage the status to negotiate a great deal including offering to pay the move-out cost for the buyer.
- Able to get an excellent deal because the pre-foreclosure seller is a distressed seller—distressed properties typically sell for a discount to facilitate a faster deal.
- Buying homes in pre-foreclosure allows investor /buyers to acquire property with large equity.

2. The Auction Stage: The lender can sell the property at a public auction to the highest bidder after advertising it in a designated newspaper for four weeks. Here, the investor could participate in the bidding and determine if he can get a deal. Usually, the bidding starts at the mortgage amount. You, the investor, have to do your homework to make sure you are getting a great deal. If there are no successful bidders, the lender can take the property as collateral for the loan and sell the property at a future date.

Strategies for Buying in a Foreclosure Auction

- Find and track foreclosure auctions. Online platforms, such as auction.com and realtytrac.com can help you locate and bid on foreclosure auctions.

- Remember to research the property. This is crucial; you want to know if there are any liens or encumbrances on the property. You also want to conduct a comparable analysis to make sure the property is a good deal.
- Scout the area and drive by to determine if you like the area. I have always maintained that when you buy a property, you are really buying the neighborhood.
- Make sure you have obtained financing for the purchase.
- Confirm all auction details even a day before the auction. Sometimes, at the last minute, the bank will withdraw or cancel the sale.

After you have done all your due diligence, it is time to attend the auction and bid on the property of your choice. The winning bid will receive a certificate of title.

3. Post-Foreclosure Bargains—Real Estate Owned: REO refers to property owned by a lender—often a bank, credit union, or quasi-governmental entity—that has not been successfully sold at a foreclosure auction. If the property is not sold at the auction, the bank reclaims the property and puts it in its resale inventory. Banks generally sell the foreclosed properties through asset management companies. Asset management companies contract real estate brokerage firms to sell these properties. The key is to align yourself with an investor-friendly agent to send you some of these bargain properties. HUD properties, Fannie Mae, Freddie Mac, and others fall under this REO category.

The federal government also sells foreclosed properties on such websites as:

- Hud Homestore (www.hudhomestore.com): Housing and Urban Development (HUD) homes are foreclosed properties that were originally purchased with Federal Housing Administration (FHA) loans.
- Federal Home Loan Mortgage Corporation (www.homesteps.com): Federal Home Loan Mortgage Corporation (FHLMC or Freddie Mac) is a government-owned corporation that buys mortgages and packages them into mortgage-backed securities. Banks use the funds received from Freddie Mac to make new loans to homebuyers. The website to find FHLMC foreclosed homes is www.homesteps.com.
- Federal National Mortgage Association (www.homepath.com): The Federal National Mortgage Association (FNMA), typically known as Fannie Mae, is a government-sponsored enterprise established to stimulate the housing market by making more mortgages available to moderate- to low-income buyers.

My Observation

Many are under the impression that it is automatically an excellent deal when a property is sold as a foreclosure. One has to do an analysis and due diligence based on your investment strategy to make sure such deals are prudent.

14

Understanding the Short Sale Process

A short sale occurs when homeowners sell their property for less than the amount due on the mortgage.

An example: A buyer took out a home mortgage loan for $350,000 several years ago. However, due to unforeseen financial difficulties, he fell behind on his monthly payments. To make matters worse, a severe deterioration in the housing market caused the value of his home to plummet to $200,000, while his mortgage stood at $300,000. In this scenario, the shortfall is $100,000.

A short sale is always initiated by the homeowner. Its financial consequences are less severe than those of a foreclosure. For the investor/buyer, it's important to calculate costs and to be sure there is room for profit when the house is resold.

Short Sales: Your Opportunities

The short sale process is a tedious, complicated process, but if you master it, there is big money to be made.

As an investor buying a short sale property, you can help the seller prepare their paperwork as well as your proposal to buy the short-sale property. The seller's documentation to the bank includes:

- Request for mortgage assistance
- Hardship letter—a hardship letter explaining the circumstances that are preventing you from making your mortgage payments
- Payroll stubs
- Listing agreement—short-sale contract
- Short-sale rider
- Contractor estimates of repairs—comparable properties
- Distressed financial status

Most short-sale properties are listed on real estate websites. Some listings may not read "short sale," so you might have to look for clues within the listing, such as "subject to bank approval" or "give the bank time to respond."

You should know that short sales can take weeks or months for lender approval. Many buyers who submit an offer end up canceling because of the delay. As a short-sale investor, you have to be ready for long waits for bank approval. Rules for short-sale transactions vary from state to state, but the steps usually include:

- Short-sale package—the borrower has to prove financial hardship by submitting a package that includes financial statements, a letter describing the seller's hardship(s), and financial records, including tax returns, W-2s, payroll stubs, and bank statements.
- Short-sale offer—once a seller accepts an offer from a potential buyer, the listing agent or the investor sends the lender the listing agreement, an executed purchase offer, the buyer's pre-approval letter, a copy of the earnest money check, and the seller's short-sale package. If the package is missing anything—either because a document wasn't submitted or due to a filing error on the bank's part (e.g., the bank lost it), the process will be delayed.

- Bank processing—the bank's review of the offer can take several weeks to months. It's important to note that just because the seller accepts an offer doesn't mean the bank will agree to the price. If the bank thinks it can make more money through foreclosure proceedings, it can reject the bid.

Numbers Tell the Story

It is said that the money is made "in the buy," meaning that a reasonable purchase price is often the key to a successful deal. If you can get a property for a good price, you increase the odds of coming out ahead when it's time to sell. If the purchase price is on the high end, on the other hand, you'll likely watch your profit margin erode.

You should be able to buy the property, put it in excellent condition, and sell it at a price where you can still make a profit. Investors need to sell the house quickly—typically at below-market—and a good purchase price makes this possible.

The purchase price is only one important number, however. You'll have to make some other calculations as well, including:

- Repair and renovation costs.
- Material, labor, permits, inspection fees, trash removal, storage costs, and dumpster rentals.
- Unforeseen costs. I always recommend an inspection before making the purchase. A cracked foundation, faulty wiring, or extensive termite damage may be a deal killer.
- After repair value. ARV is an estimate of the property's fair market value after any repairs and renovations are made. As an investor in short sales, you have to look at this number to determine whether a property has profit potential. The best way to evaluate a property's ARV is to look at the

comparables, or comps—homes that have recently sold in the area (typically up to a mile away from the subject property) with similar features in terms of square footage, number of bedrooms and bathrooms.

- Carrying costs. Your expenses for holding onto the property. The longer you own the property, the more you will spend in carrying costs—mortgage payments (including interest); property taxes; insurance; condo and association fees; utilities (electric, gas, water, sewer, trash).

Determine Profitability

For an investment to be profitable, the sum of your costs (purchase price, repair and renovation costs, and carrying costs) must be lower than the ARV. If your costs are close to or higher than the ARV, it will be difficult or impossible to make a profit. You can determine the potential profit by subtracting the purchase price, repair and renovation (R&R) costs, and carrying costs from the ARV, for example:

Profit = $600,000 – $250,000 – $15000 – $36000
Profit = ARV – Purchase Price – R&R Costs – Carrying Costs
Real estate investors expect a 30 percent gross profit on a property. (Use the 70 percent rule.)

- 70% of the $600,000 = $450,000
- Gross profit = $600,000 - $450,000 = $150,000

The Bottom Line

A short-sale property can provide an excellent opportunity to purchase a house for less money. In many cases, short-sale homes are in reasonable condition. While the purchase price might be higher than a foreclosure, the costs of making the home marketable can be much lower, and the disadvantages to the seller less severe. However, because of the lengthy process, buyers and sellers must be willing to wait.

While many investors purchase short-sale properties and quickly resell them for a profit, others choose to maintain ownership and use the property for income by collecting rent. In either case, each property must be carefully evaluated prior to purchase to determine if it has profit potential.

Because tax laws are complicated and can change from time to time, it is always recommended that you consult with a certified public accountant (CPA) who knows about real estate investing and related tax laws to give you comprehensive and up-to-date information. It can mean the difference between making a profit and taking a loss.

NOTE: As an agent, you can specialize in short sales and receive the designation from the National Association of Realtors (NAR). Holders of this certification—Short Sales and Foreclosure designation (SFR)—have received specialized training in short sales and foreclosures, qualifying sellers for short sales, negotiating with lenders, and protecting buyers.

15

Understanding Mortgage Notes Investing

R eal estate note investing is the process of buying mortgage notes to generate a profit. When you buy a property, you secure a loan and make monthly payments on it. That's a real estate note. These notes are actively traded behind the scenes. It is not uncommon to receive a letter from a different company after buying a property that your payment should be sent elsewhere. Your loan was simply sold to another lender.

Another essential fact is that owner-financing deals are a growing trend in real estate financing. In 2019, an estimated 86,155 seller-financed first-position notes* was created. The dollar volume was $23.9 billion. One can participate in buying notes from private individuals instead of institutional sellers.

Note investing is an area that is a mystery to a lot of people, including real estate agents. Investing in real estate notes is a unique alternative to acquiring and owning properties. It is possible for a note investor to generate a passive income stream as part of his portfolio.

I was introduced to note investing early in my real estate investing career when I sold my first investment property through

---

* Mortgages that are in first position have the highest claim. The first position will always be paid before any claim on the mortgage or the note.

owner financing. When I sold my property, I carried the promissory note on the property for the buyer. The buyer was paying me monthly income on the note, and when I needed a lump sum of money, I decided to sell my promissory note at a discount to a note investor.

What Is a Promissory Note?

A promissory note (often just called a "note") is a formal debt from a borrower promising to repay a debt. The note spells out the loan terms, and the borrower signs it to indicate their consent.

The borrower and the lender; the amount borrowed; the interest rate; the repayment schedule; the date and location of issuance. What happens in the case of the borrower defaulting?

Once the borrower issues the note, the lender holds on to it while the loan is outstanding. Any time before the borrower makes the last payment, the lender can trade or sell the note. Once the borrower fully pays off the loan, the creditor marks the note as "paid in full" and returns it to the borrower.

Mortgage notes are associated with home loans and secured by the real estate purchased. When you buy a property, you typically sign two documents: the mortgage agreement or deeds of trust and a promissory note. The promissory note records the loan terms; the mortgage or deed of trust secures it with the real estate you're purchasing. The lender will record their lien by filing the mortgage at the county land records office, but they'll hang on to the note.

Investing in real estate notes is generally the purchase of an existing mortgage. And when you purchase a mortgage note, you become the lender and have all the lender's rights. You don't own the real estate, but you have a right to take the collateral if the borrower doesn't pay.

Purchasing mortgage notes is a very lucrative alternative to actually buying and investing in actual properties. Unlike hard real estate purchases, you don't own any property with a note-based strategy.

With a note-based strategy, you invest in a debt secured by real estate and not actual real property.

One can purchase notes on the secondary market, where the trading of securities occurs. The secondary market consists of both equity and debt markets.

What that market looks like depends on whether you want to take a risk on a non-performing note or play it safe(r) with a performing one.

Here are the differences between those two types of notes:

Non-Performing Notes: This is a mortgage loan in which the borrower is not complying with the terms of the note. Non-performing loans encompass borrowers who are thirty days or more behind on their mortgage. Investing in non-performing notes comes with a higher return on investment (ROI) but carries higher risk.

Performing Notes: A mortgage loan in which the borrower is following the terms of the note. Essentially, the borrower is not missing any payments. Purchasing notes for mortgages with a steady track record of on-time payments are generally safer and less-involved investments. The appeal of performing notes is that investors can start receiving payments almost immediately—minimal effort required. However, since these loans make money, you won't get as big of a discount as you would for a non-performing loan, so your ROI will usually be lower.

The reasons investors are drawn to real estate notes vary, depending on their investment strategy. An appealing feature of performing real estate notes to many investors is the hands-off nature of the purchase. Because you don't own property, you don't have to deal with tenants or property managers, make repairs, or worry about city codes. You just get to kick back, put up your feet, and collect the borrower's payments.

When you invest in real estate notes, you get all the advantages of being a lender, without the headaches of being a landlord. And you have a lien that collateralizes your investment.

The Benefits of Note Investing

No Property Management: Many investors have turned to real estate to create cash flow, but managing rental properties can be time-consuming and riddled with problems. Being the lender means you receive the income while someone else manages the property.

No Maintenance Issues: As a lender, all maintenance is the responsibility of the homeowner.

No Managing Tenants: Whereas rental property owners are concerned about vacancies in their rentals, the homeowner must continue paying the mortgage—or you can take back the property through foreclosure.

Lien Secured by Real Estate: Mortgage notes are secured by the property, meaning if a borrower suddenly stopped paying their mortgage, you have the right to foreclose and take back the property.

Passive Income: If you do your underwriting correctly, we haven't found many investments that can provide income that is as passive as mortgage notes.

Liquid Secondary Market: This means there is a strong market for mortgage notes, which allows investors to sell their notes without incurring the selling costs or opportunity cost of exiting real estate.

Discount: Perhaps the greatest advantage of investing in mortgage notes is the discount at which buyers can purchase notes. As mentioned earlier, banks generally aren't well equipped for these types of notes. Discounts create higher yields, greater profits when paid off, and additional capital protection.

Where to Find Notes

1. www.paperstac.com—the website is a note intermediary
2. www.notesellerlist.com—an advanced seller data service
3. http://www.noteinvesting.com—number one source for note-investing information

You can enter the note-investing field by buying into a mortgage note fund. Many investors prefer a more passive approach in this asset class and partner with fund managers. By doing this, you don't need to manage the assets actively, you diversify your risk across many investments and geographies, and you leverage the expertise of their team. Fund managers are experienced managers with a track record and experience in real estate.

16

Avoiding the Ten
Mistakes Investors Make

R eal estate investing is complex, and you should approach
with a definite plan and strategy. Investing in real estate
property can become a very appealing idea—either as a full-time
business endeavor or a great part-time undertaking. Realize the
rewards of your efforts will be very profitable if you approach real
estate investing the right way.

Here are ten potential traps to avoid as you contemplate starting your investment in real estate.

1. Lack of investment knowledge: In real estate investing,
   the risk involved is directly proportional to your
   knowledge. As an investor, you have to invest in your
   education by attending seminars and other
   educational opportunities before you plunge into the
   game. The more knowledge you have, the more
   confidence you will have. The more you know about
   negotiation, creative real estate financing, lease
   options, different acquisition techniques, and other
   strategies, the less risky your investment becomes.
2. Lack of an investment strategy: What is your plan?
   Are you a cash flow investor or a rehab investor? It

is advisable to devise your strategy before you buy; it will enable you to see your financial numbers clearly. Many beginning investors do not have a clear plan, and they lose money because they try to change strategy in midcourse.

3. Misunderstanding the real estate market: Even if you buy only one property per year, pay attention to shifts in the marketplace. An interplay of market economic conditions do influence the local real estate market, such as shifts in population, immigration patterns, inventory of new buildings compared to re-sales, foreclosure levels in the marketplace, interest rate levels. The inflow of Wall Street money into the real estate market has made a tremendous impact. As investors, we need to understand market forces to make rational decisions. For instance, if you are buying and flipping, the current interest rate environment is suitable for high-end luxury homes because interest rates are at historic lows.

4. Being too greedy: Many investors come to this business wanting to get rich on their first deal. Investing and building wealth does not have to be doing a quick deal here and a quick deal there. Some investors have told me they wanted to make $30,000 on their first deal. This belies the lack of a strategy for making this kind of money. My suggestion is that we have to be realistic in our approach to real estate investment. Like any worthwhile business, it takes a while to succeed and make a lot of money.

5. Unfamiliarity with financing options: Financing is the wheel that turns the real estate industry. As an investor, it behooves you to learn and know about this topic. Financing affects real estate values. Interest rates are a very determinate factor in real

estate financing. The higher the interest rate, the higher the monthly payment and vice versa—the lower the interest rate, the lower the mortgage interest you can afford. There are many options available to the real estate investor—from the ubiquitous traditional financing to the more esoteric creative real estate financing. It is advisable to seek the advice and services of an aggressive, knowledgeable, and investor-savvy mortgage lender to help you with your financing needs.

6. Lack of capital: Real estate investment is very capital intensive. I have always cautioned beginning investors to have some cushion to carry them through the lean times and in case of unexpected and occasional problems that often accompany rental properties. As the saying goes, it is not advisable to be cash-poor and equity-rich. Many investors place heavy emphasis on the quantity of the property they possess instead of the quality of their portfolio. One prominent investor recently suggested that investors should grade their holdings every year to get rid of all nonperformers.

7. Not treating real estate investment as a business: The truth is, like any other business, it takes time for a real estate investing business to develop a life of its own, to define your niche, and even acquire the necessary capital to complete deals. Plan on about two to five years to develop a sound system. It takes months, even years, to build a sustainable infrastructure to support and nurture your real estate business.

8. No winning strategy: This can be as simple as devising a set of rules to achieve your investment goals. As an investor, you should be able to quantify your winning formula. For example, my winning

formula is buying wholesale properties and reselling them to other investors, generating at least $10,000 per transaction. A winning formula is designed to marshal your resources, seen and unseen.

9. Naïve about investment psychology: It has to do with your mindset as an investor. As a real estate investor, most of your offers will be rejected because you want to buy your properties wholesale or below market price. Therefore, you have to prepare yourself mentally for all the rejections, or you will quit the game of real estate investing after a number of your offers have been rejected.

10. No exit strategy: As an investor, you have to know your exit strategy before you buy. Are you buying the property to flip and sell to other investors? Are you buying, rehabbing, and selling to another investor or the retail buyer? There are nine exit strategies: rent, rent-to-own, lease purchase, lease option, sandwich lease, "subject to," land contract, contract for deed, wraparound mortgage, and assumptions.

17

The Ten Building Blocks of a Profitable Real Estate Investment

Building wealth through real estate is achievable. There are different strategies you can employ to achieve your aim. However, regardless of your chosen strategy to real estate investing, these ten building blocks should serve as a guide to help you navigate the real estate strategy that you have chosen.

1. Education: Real estate is a vast and complex subject that you need to allocate time to study. Fortunately, there are many channels available for you to explore and learn. They include:
    a. Books on real estate
    b. Blogs (BiggerPockets, platform)
    c. Real estate forums
    d. Networking—Real Estate Investors Association
    e. Seminars
    f. Webinars
    g. Podcasts
    h. Mentors
    i. Continuing education at colleges and universities
    j. REI-USA—premier online real estate education

2. Winning formula: Rules you devise to help you achieve your investment goals.

    a.   Niche: The kinds of properties you will buy— single-family, multi-family, commercial, industrial, vacant lots.

    b.   Strategy: How are you buying them and your exit strategy? Are you buying to wholesale? Are you buying, fixing to sell? Are you buying to hold for the long term? (You should consider how your strategy will fit your overall financial goals.)

3. Understanding the local market: If possible, take the real estate agency course in your area—it will help you know more about real estate in general and your potential market in particular. It is advisable to be current with the interplay of market economic forces so you can make intelligent decisions about your real estate business.

4.Develop a team: Real estate is a team sport, and you need different experts to help you achieve your goals. A complete team might include an attorney, preferably one who buys properties for his portfolio; appraiser; real estate agent who specializes In investment properties; title/escrow company (stay away from big-name companies, find one that caters to small investors); insurance agent from a company that insures properties; an aggressive CPA who owns real estate; a reputable, honest contractor who will give you free estimates; a savvy, creative, mortgage broker who is experienced with investors; more than one money partner; an experienced home inspector; and, last but not least, a mentor to offer helpful counsel and advice.

5. Secure capital to complete deals from:

    a.   Banks

  b. Mortgage brokers and mortgage bankers

  c. Hard money lenders (They will loan you 70 percent of the after repair value. If the ARV is $100,000, they will lend you $70,000, including repairs.)

  d. OPM, a.k.a. other people's money

  e. 401K (This can be used to fund your real estate deals.)

  f. Front money partners (They become partners in your transaction.)

6. Know your exit strategy: The way you market your properties is intertwined with the financial options available to you as an investor. The more options you have and know about alternative marketing methods through creative real estate financing strategies, the more effective you will become as a real estate investor.

7. Know the tax implications of your deals: The way you structure your deals will affect your tax situation. For example, if you are just buying and selling, your profit is considered an ordinary income and you are taxed at the higher effective tax rate. If you buy and hold your property long term, it is considered passive income and taxed differently. Know the three kinds of income: ordinary, passive, and portfolio. It is also advisable to be familiar with 1031 Exchanges,* which involve swapping one investment property for another in a way that allows capital gains taxes to be deferred.

8. Know the risk involved: There is risk involved in real estate, but it does not have to be risky. Are you risk

---

* 1031 Exchanges: From Section 1031 of the US Internal Revenue Code, which allows you to avoid paying capital gains taxes when you sell an investment property and reinvest the proceeds within certain time limits on similar property of equal or greater value.

averse or risk tolerant? Before you buy property, you have to analyze it thoroughly and your plans for the property after the purchase. Your exit strategy will determine your purchase price. There are specific financial formulas for analyzing properties. It is possible to minimize the risk by being more knowledgeable

9. Time: It takes a long time to learn and understand real estate investment, but it is one of the avenues that will catapult you to enormous wealth with time. At best, you have to give yourself time to grow and mature. It may take five to ten years for you to be seasoned as a real estate investor and know the options available to you as an investor. But it's worth every minute you put into the process.

10. Real estate is the IDEAL investment: Remember the acronym—Income, Depreciation, Equity, Appreciation, Leverage.

18

The Investor—My Personal Investment Philosophy

I have had the opportunity to participate in numerous real estate investment transactions over the past thirty years. These are some ideas and principles that I have developed over the years.

1. Passion: It is imperative that you love what you do. I believe this will carry you through the difficult periods that will confront you as an investor.
2. Integrity: People will do business with you when you are a man of your word. I raised considerable amounts of money with my front money partners because they trusted me with their money.
3. Know the rules of the game: It is crucial to recognize the difference between a cash flow deal and a cash-out strategy. This enables you to structure your offer accordingly.
4. Return on Investment: This is a measurement of how effective you are structuring your deals. For example, if you put in $10,000 and net $20,000, your ROI is 50 percent.
5. Know your intended profit before you buy: You buy

a property because you are making the profit today, not five years from today. This is why you have to analyze the deal carefully. This method prevents you from speculating on what might happen tomorrow; you do not know whether real estate prices will continue to appreciate.

6. Learn to Leverage: Leverage uses small efforts to produce big results—something that you use to gain maximum advantage. Leverage gives us exponential growth in our investment activities. For example, when buying a property, one can put down $5,000 to control real estate valued at $100,000. Time and people can be leveraged too. For example, an investor using an agent to locate investment properties is a form of leverage; another is using front-money partners to finance your deal.

7. Investment is not emotions, just numbers: To a deal maker and real estate investor, all that matters are the numbers. If they look right, go ahead and make an offer. Don't fall prey to paralysis by analysis. Before you inspect a piece of property, make sure the numbers are correct.

8. Ride the winners and cut your losers: If an investment is not doing well, try to sell it and minimize your losses. This will happen in your deal-making process, and you just have to get used to it; you will not win all the time. Sometimes you will make mistakes, no matter how seasoned you are. You have to be mentally prepared for setbacks.

9. Know your niche: Somebody once said, "There are riches in niches." Defining your niche means that you have specific properties that you are buying and selling. You know the characteristics and profile of your buyers. You're aiming for a well-defined target market.

10. Do market research: This enables you to define your market and approach it intelligently. In my case, I focus on working with real estate investors.

11. Time: It is advisable not to draw broad conclusions from early results. In fact, a good measure of an investor's accomplishments might take five to ten years. Real estate is a vast field with many opportunities to achieve extraordinary financial rewards.

12. Action: When the time is ripe, you have to act. Seize all opportunities to make a move and "just do it." Do not analyze a deal so much so that you are unable to act.

13. Put a system together: Systems enable you to become more efficient. The more repetition you have, the more your actions become automatic. This improves your efficiency.

19

My Insights into Real Estate Investment and Entrepreneurship

I have always enjoyed the entrepreneurial life. Through my real estate investment career and the various businesses I have started, acquired, and operated over the years, I have developed these insights that I want to share with you.

1. Know your assets: Wealth creation involves how you think about money and your role in making it happen. As I acquired the wealth-building mentality, I was attracted to businesses and investments that generated income. Even as a cab driver, I knew that my asset was my vehicle, which I had to maintain and manage its income.

2. Learn how to save: In my cab-driving career, I knew that I had to tap into my resources if my cab needed repairs. I saved enough money to operate my business—and pay my way through college. I graduated debt-free from Baruch College, City University of New York in Manhattan.

3. Learn to be thrifty: Amid today's extravagant lifestyles, advising people to be thrifty seems to be bucking the trend. I say, though, spend money only

where necessary for the success of your enterprise. Avoid expenditures that do not add to the growth of your company.

The habitually thrifty person will recognize opportunities for reducing overhead. Minor savings can mean a great deal, even representing the difference between a net profit and a net loss. There is always a fluid reserve to meet contingencies; carry one through the slack period or make it possible to expand or make improvements without resorting to borrowing.

4. Accumulate capital: The art of being thrifty helped me accumulate capital and deploy my accumulated resources. This led me to the study of real estate investing. Soon after, I bought my first investment property in Brooklyn, New York, and a second one in Jersey City.

5. Develop basic business skills: I developed a platform for a lifetime of entrepreneurial activity. I bought a business and started another one from scratch. From this, I developed real estate investment and business courses for colleges and universities, where I taught in their continuing education programs for more than ten years.

6. Know your customers: I was friendly and kind to my fares, which generated more business. (Some customers contacted me personally for routine trips.) I made a lot of tips as a result of my excellent customer service.

7. Manage your workload: I always worked with the amount of money I had to make and would make that amount before I stopped working, which helped increase my earnings. When I needed extra money, I would drive extra hours so that my reserve funds were untouched.

8. Learn how to handle adversity: Do not assume that everything is rosy just because you started a business or investment. Business is fraught with risk and adversity. There will be times when you will feel like quitting, but if you love what you are doing and have a passion for it, this will sustain you. When driving my cab in New York City in the early 1970s, I was robbed at gunpoint several times. Of course, that got me thinking about quitting, but I had no alternative but to continue the business and be careful about who I picked up.

9. Work on your endurance and stamina: To be at your peak performance, you need to keep yourself in the best possible mental and physical condition. To minimize stress and its attendant problems, incorporate fitness and exercise into your routine. It does not make sense to succumb to stress or the effects of overwork in pursuit of your goal. Schedule yourself in such a way that you can get enough rest and maintain a cheerful, positive, mental outlook.

10. Become self-motivated: As an entrepreneur, you are responsible for every step of your achievements. Sometimes I did not feel like going on the road and hustling for customers. Nor did I have a boss. I had to learn to be self-motivated, how to operate the business and make money. You must be able to work alone on every task toward your goal. However, you still need to assemble experts in other fields, such as accounting and legal, to help you realize your dream. You're in charge of gathering facts and making quick decisions. Your success as an entrepreneur and real estate investor will depend mainly on the quality of decisions you make and how you act on them.

20

Principles of Asset Protection

After you have started acquiring properties, you need to protect your assets. Individuals and businesses use asset protection techniques to limit creditors' access to certain valuable assets while operating within the bounds of the law.

After years of building your portfolio and acquiring a sizable net worth, it is time to protect yourself against lawsuits and other calamities.

Here are three elements to use to protect yourself and your business:

1. Insurance

This is the most popular asset protection strategy in the real estate industry. The coverage you choose for your property depends on the real estate type. You can protect your home with a homeowner's policy and your commercial property with a business policy.

You'll need to increase your coverage as your portfolio enlarges. Ultimately, consider an umbrella policy for comprehensive coverage. Insurance will protect you against numerous catastrophic events.

2. Limited Liability

Forming a limited liability company for rental property can

protect your personal assets from potential lawsuits. With limited liability, debtors can't come for your home as compensation for the issues arising in your business. The corporation pays for its expenses. You can buy a house with an LLC and rent it to yourself to minimize financial risks. This strategy will limit the chances of personal real estate asset seizure. But you must be keen on asset transfers to avoid practices that could be considered fraudulent. Have your commercial properties in different LLCs. When one asset faces a risk, the rest of your property will be safe. You can have your real estate investments in other names to avoid adverse effects when you're subject to a lawsuit.

3. Land Trust

This legal entity takes ownership of, or authority over, a property at the owner's request. Land trusts are living trusts that allow for the management of property while the owner remains alive. Each land trust's terms are unique and can be tailored to individual needs.

In a trust, your name does not have to appear on records. When caught up in a lawsuit, lawyers can't connect your trust to any of your property. Putting your house in a trust will protect your investment.

Land trusts have three essential parts—the grantor, trustee, and beneficiary. The grantor is the person who creates the trust and transfers the property; the trustee manages the trust; the beneficiary is the one who benefits from the trust.

Acknowledgments

The idea of writing a book has always fascinated me. I have always dreamed of being an author and I am grateful for the opportunity to write this book.

I would like to express my sincere appreciation and thanks to Mr. Peter Giant Bowleg of Black Eagle Group LLC for his encouraging words. Peter is an author and publisher himself, and as soon as I expressed an interest in writing a book, he sent me an email outlining what I needed to do to complete and publish the book.

I also want to thank Mr. Jim Davis of Type Right Editing for his expertise in the editorial edit and making the book much more coherent to read. His suggestions and input were very invaluable!

The publishers and editors at BookLogix were very encouraging and professional. To my art/cover designer, Scot Mmobuosi, thank you!

I will also thank friends and family who in their own way encouraged me.

Finally, to my wife Vena Ansong, for first reading the manuscript and working on the first draft. Your love and unwavering support of all my business ventures has led to the accomplishment of this goal. Thank You!

COMMON
FINANCIAL TERMS

You can improve your knowledge about financial and real estate matters by becoming familiar with financial terminology or its lingo. Try to spend an hour a day studying financial terms — until you're intimate with them.

1031 Exchange: From Section 1031 of the US Internal Revenue Code, which allows you to avoid paying capital gains taxes when you sell an investment property and reinvest the proceeds within certain time limits on similar property of equal or greater value.

Addendum: An attachment to a contract, often to describe required inspections or financing terms.

Amenity Value: A property's favorable traits, such as being in a good neighborhood with quality schools, parks, and playgrounds.

Amortized Loan: A loan in which the principal payments are paid in certain specified, usually equal, installments.

Appraisal: An estimate or opinions of value, usually for loan or tax purposes.

Asset Management: Determining a client's portfolio and

direction by a financial services institution, usually an investment bank or an individual. Institutions offer investment services along with a wide range of traditional and alternative product offerings.

Assets Under Management (AUM): The total market value of the investments that a person or entity manages on behalf of clients. Assets Under Management definitions and formulas vary by company. In the calculation of AUM, some financial institutions include bank deposits, mutual funds, and cash in their calculation.

Assign: To transfer to another claim, a right, or a title to a property.

Assumption: The act of assuming or taking over the primary liability for payment of an existing mortgage or trust deed.

Balloon Payment: The final payment on a note that is greater than the preceding installments. Real estate law dictates that any final payment be twice as much as the smallest installment payment.

Bandit sign: A poster-sized sign that real estate investors often use as a marketing tool and can often be seen on street corners with verbiage such as "We buy houses. Cash."

Binder: A payment made to hold property pending mortgage approval. Such an amount is determined by what is acceptable to the seller. (In some circumstances, it is 1 percent of the sale price.)

Cash Flow: Net amount of cash and cash equivalents being transferred into and out of a business. Cash received represents inflows, while money spent represents outflows.

Cloud on a Title: A Cloud on a Title is a claim or encumbrance that affects property ownership. These claims or encumbrances can arise from easements or mortgages on the land. They can also occur from a deed or a lien defect that may yield title to a third party, such as mechanic's liens.

Contract for Deed: A tool allowing buyers who don't qualify for traditional lending or who want faster financing to purchase a property. Under a Contract for Deed, the buyer makes regular payments to the seller until the amount owed is paid in full or the buyer finds another means to pay off the balance.

Caveat Emptor: "Let the buyer beware," an expression once used in real estate to put the burden of an undisclosed defect on the buyer. This concept has been discarded in most states.

Contract of Sale: A contract that assigns property to the buyer; title remains with the seller until the contract has been fulfilled.

Closing: Buyer and seller meet to finalize the sale of property and transfer of title.

Collateral: The property is subject to security interest.

Collateral Loan: Lender places a claim against borrower's property as security for loan repayment.

Compound Interest: A loan or deposit interest amount calculated by the initial principal and the accumulated interest from previous periods.

Commitment Letter: Written pledge or promise, a firm agreement that often describes the terms of a mortgage loan.

Conditional Sales Contract: Written agreement for the sale of property stating that the seller retains title until the conditions of the contract have been fulfilled.

Depreciation: In accounting, allocation of the cost of an asset over its estimated useful life. In appraisal, a charge against the re-production cost (new) of an asset for its estimated wear and obsolescence. Depreciation may be physical, functional, or economic.

Default: Missing the deadline by which a debt must be paid. (e.g., If the note is due and payable by January 1, then on January 2, 1999, that note is in default.)

Due-on-Sale Clause: Provision in a mortgage that states that a loan is due upon the sale of the property.

Easement: Right, privilege, or interest that one party has in the land of another. The most common easements are for utility lines.

Encroachment: Building, a part of a building, or an obstruction that physically intrudes upon, overlaps, or trespasses upon the property of another.

Encumbrance: Any right to or interest in land that affects its value. This includes outstanding mortgage loans, unpaid taxes, easements, and deed restrictions.

Equity of Redemption: The right of the borrower to regain property, generally after default but before foreclosure.

Equity: The value of property beyond the total amount owed on it.

Escrow: Money placed in a bank or with a third party until certain conditions are met.

Factoring: A method of financing in which a manufacturer sells account receivables at a discount. Also, a funding source agrees to pay a company the value of an invoice minus a discount for commission and fees.

Floating Rate Loan: An interest rate that moves up and down with the market or an index. It can also be referred to as a variable interest rate because it can vary throughout the debt obligation.

Fixed Interest Rate: The interest rate of a debt obligation stays constant for the duration of the loan's term. (e.g., If you have a loan at 2 percent over the prime rate and the prime changes from 7 to 7.25 percent, your interest rate will change from 9 to 9.25 percent.) This is also known as a variable rate loan.

Foreclosure: Termination of all rights of a mortgage or the grantee in the property covered by the mortgage.

Garnishment: A withholding of wages for repayment of debt.

General Partner: One of two or more investors who jointly own a business and assume a day-to-day role in managing it.

Gross Rent Multiplier: A measure of the value of an investment property. It is calculated by dividing the property's sale price by its gross annual rental income.

Hard Money Loan: A loan that is secured by real property. Hard money loans are considered loans of "last resort," or short-term or bridge loans. These loans are primarily used in real estate transactions, with the lender generally being individuals or companies and not banks.

Hypothecate: To pledge property to another as security for a loan without transferring possession or title.

Installment Loan: A loan contract in which repayments are made in equal installments.

Interest: Amount a lender charges for using assets expressed as a percentage of the principal or total amount of the debt. The interest rate is typically noted annually, known as the annual percentage rate (APR). The assets borrowed could include cash, consumer goods, or significant assets such as vehicles or buildings.

Investment: An asset or item acquired to generate income or appreciation. Appreciation refers to an increase in the value of an asset over time. When an individual purchases goods as an investment, the intent is not to consume the goods but rather to use them in the future to create wealth. Investment always involves the outlay of some asset today—time, money, or effort—in hopes of a greater payoff in the future than what was initially put in.

Jointly and Severally Liable: More than one person personally guaranteeing a loan. When such language appears in a contract, each borrower is liable for the entire amount. As a practicable matter, if the loan is in default, the lender will attempt to collect the whole amount from the individual.

Judicial Foreclosure: Foreclosure is used when no sale power is present in the mortgage or deed of trust. Generally, after the court declares a foreclosure, the property will be auctioned off to the highest bidder. The process takes place through the court system.

Land banking: Practice of aggregating parcels of land for future sale or development.

Land Contract: A form of seller financing, similar to a mortgage.

But rather than borrowing money from a lender or bank to buy real estate, the buyer makes payments to the owner or seller until the purchase price is fully paid.

Land Trust: Legal entity that assumes control over property and other real estate assets at the behest of the property's owner. It's a living trust, which is generally revocable, meaning the terms of the trust can be changed or terminated at any time.

Lien: A claim on property as security for a debt.

Limited Liability Company: An LLC is a business structure in which its owners are not personally liable for its debts or liabilities. Limited liability companies are hybrid entities that combine the characteristics of a corporation with those of a partnership or sole proprietorship.

Line of Credit: A lending limit established by a lender allowing the borrower to access funds to the limit at any time as permitted by the lender.

Liquidity: Amount of assets that are readily convertible to cash.

Loan-to-Value Ratio: An amount borrowed as a percentage of the cost or value of the property purchased. Typically, loan assessments with high LTV ratios are considered higher-risk loans. There, if the mortgage is approved, the loan has a higher interest rate.

Mortgage: A contract for a debt that uses real estate as security.

Mortgage Broker: A mortgage broker works as an intermediary between you and lenders. In other words, mortgage brokers don't control the borrowing guidelines, timeline, or final loan approval. Brokers are licensed professionals who collect your mortgage application and qualifying documentation and counsel you on items to address in your credit report and with your finances to strengthen your approval chances. Many mortgage brokers work for an independent mortgage company, so they can shop multiple lenders on your behalf, helping you find the best possible rate and deal. Mortgage brokers are typically paid by the lender after a loan closes; sometimes, the borrower pays the broker's commission up front at closing.

Mortgage Lender: A mortgage lender is a financial institution or mortgage bank that offers and underwrites home loans. Lenders have specific borrowing guidelines to verify your creditworthiness and ability to repay a loan. They set the terms, interest rate, repayment schedule, and other vital aspects of your mortgage.

Non-Judicial Foreclosure: A process where a lender can foreclose on your home without filing suit or appearing in court before a judge.

Perfect a Lien: File legal documents to ensure a lien is on file with the appropriate municipal authorities (generally town, city, county clerk, or registry of deeds for mortgages).

Personal Guarantee: An individual's legal promise to repay credit issued to a business they serve as an executive or partner. If a business becomes unable to repay the debt, the individual assumes personal responsibility for the balance. Personal guarantees provide an extra level of protection to credit issuers who want to make sure they will be repaid. Banks require a guarantee by the majority of owners. A personal guarantee means you are liable until the debt is fully paid. This is true with all business loans except to large companies with substantial worth and widespread ownership.

Personal Loan: Amount of money you can borrow for a variety of purposes. For instance, you may use a personal loan to consolidate debt, pay for home renovations, or plan a dream wedding. Personal loans can be offered by banks, credit unions, or online lenders. The money you borrow must be repaid within a specific time, typically with interest. Some lenders may also charge fees for personal loans.

Personal Property: Any property that is not land or attached to land, such as an automobile, stocks, bonds, inventory used in business, machinery, furniture.

Pledge: To deliver an item to guarantee repayment of a loan. For example, one could give savings assets, life insurance policies, stock certificates, or notes as security for the loan.

Pawnshop: A business that lends money at high interest rates in exchange for collateral such as jewelry, electronic items, or anything else judged to have a resale value. The pawnshop keeps the collateral, and if the loan is repaid, the item is returned. It's an institution where property is pledged.

Points: Generally, a percentage of a number or a measurement of the change in a number—a term that is used in various contexts in financial matters. Points may indicate the interest rate on a mortgage concerning the prime lending rate or the total size of the fees attached to a mortgage. They indicate the percentage of change in the return on a bond. They also are used to report the price movements of stocks. Points are added cost frequently changed on mortgages. Payment time is typically the day you obtain a mortgage.
NOTE: Points are tax-deductible. Points are simply an added expense to the borrower. Points are expressed as a percentage. (e.g., 2 points are equal to 2 percent. For example, 2 points on a $40,000 loan is (.02 x 40,000 = $800)).

Prime Interest Rate: Rate of interest charged by banks of its most-favored commercial customers. The interest rate charged to other commercial customers is expressed as a percent or points. If the prime rate is 7 percent and you are quoted a loan at "two points over prime," your interest rate on the loan is 9 percent.

Principal: Total amount of money borrowed. The principal is the total amount of debt minus interest. It's the amount of debt on which interest is calculated.

Promissory Note: A financial instrument that contains a written promise by one party (the note's issuer or maker) to pay another party (the note's payee) a definite sum of money, either on demand or at a specified future date. A promissory note typically contains all the terms pertaining to the indebtedness, such as the principal amount, interest rate, maturity date, date and place of issuance, and issuer's signature.

Quitclaim Deed: A document that releases a person's interest in a property without stating the nature of the person's interest or rights and with no warranties of that person's interest or rights in the property. A quitclaim deed neither states nor guarantees that the person relinquishing their claim to the property had valid ownership. Still, it does prevent that person (the grantor) from later claiming they have an interest in the property. Also, it is a deed that conveys only the grantor's rights or interest in real estate without stating the nature of the rights and with no warranties of ownership.

Real Property: The land, everything that is permanently attached to the land, and all of the rights of ownership, including the right to possess, sell, lease, and enjoy the land. Real property can be classified according to its general use as residential, commercial, agricultural, industrial, or special purpose. To understand if you have the right to sell your home, you need to know which rights you possess—or don't possess.

Rentometer: A site that gives users an estimate of what rent prices are in the nearby vicinity of a subject property.

Secondary Market: A market where trading of securities is done. The secondary market consists of both equity as well as debt markets.

Security Agreement: A document that provides a lender a security interest in a specified asset or property pledged as collateral. Terms and conditions are determined at the time the security agreement is drafted. Security agreements are a necessary part of the business world, as lenders would never extend credit to certain companies without them. If the borrower defaults, the pledged collateral can be seized by the lender and sold.

Security Interest: An enforceable legal claim or lien on collateral that has been pledged, usually to obtain a loan. The borrower provides the lender with a security interest in certain assets, which gives the lender the right to repossess all or part of the property if the borrower stops making loan payments. The lender can then sell the repossessed collateral to pay off the loan.

Speculate: To invest in anything risky with the hope of making a high return on the investment.

S Corporation (S Subchapter): A type of corporation that meets specific Internal Revenue Code requirements. If it does, it may pass income (along with other credits, deductions, and losses) directly to shareholders without having to pay federal corporate taxes. Usually associated with small businesses (one hundred or fewer shareholders), S corporation status effectively gives a company the regular benefits of incorporation while enjoying the tax-exempt privileges.

Subordination: Agreeing to a secondary position as a lender in a first claim against the borrower's assets. For example, in business start-ups, if an investor loans money to a new corporation and a bank loan were also obtained, the bank would require the other lender to sign a subordination agreement.

"Subject to" Financing: An investor or purchaser takes rights to the title for a property while the seller's existing mortgage stays in place. In the simplest terms, the real estate deal is "subject to" the seller's mortgage financing the deal. "Subject to" financing is a creative way to invest in real estate.

Syndication: an investment structure in which several investors pool their capital together and invest in projects much larger than they could individually.

Voidable Contract: A formal agreement between two parties that may be rendered unenforceable for any number of legal reasons. Such reasons that can make a contract voidable may include: failure by one or both parties to disclose a material fact; a mistake, misrepresentation, or fraud; undue influence or duress.

Void Contract: A formal agreement that is effectively illegitimate and unenforceable from the moment it is created.

Wraparound Mortgage: A form of owner financing whereby the seller of property maintains an outstanding first mortgage that is then repaid in part by the new buyer. Instead of applying for a conventional bank mortgage, that buyer signs a mortgage with the seller, and the new loan is not used to pay off the seller's existing loan.

APPENDIX

THE GUT REHAB
INVESTMENT STRATEGY
AND THE COSMETIC FIXER UPPER

There are two basic investment strategies for real estate investors. There might be some variations on these two models but these two are succinct. In each of these models you have to analyze the numbers to align with the strategy you have chosen. It is in view of this that I am a strong advocate of having a "winning formula." A winning formula will help you sharpen your focus as you screen properties that fit your criteria for you make an offer:

4. The Gut Rehab Method: The strategy involves gutting the property to the bones, reconfiguring the floor space, and sometimes even adding additional bedrooms or bathrooms. The idea is to bring the interior up to contemporary standards for form and function. All mechanical systems are updated for efficiency to conform to codes and standards.

The formulas for working the numbers for a Gut Rehab Method:

THE GUT REHAB METHOD
   PROPERTY ANALYSIS FORMULA
   The Gut Rehab Method
   Maximum Retail Value - After Repair Value (ARV)

Subtract the following:

Purchase Cost   _____

Rehab Cost   _____

Holding Cost 6 Months   _____

Sales Cost (6%)   _____

Estimated Profit   _____

Contingency Factor   _____

Minimum Purchase Price   _____

Rehab Strategy: Renovate property to "dollhouse" condition including "sizzle" features. (e.g., skylights, ceiling fans, coffered/cathedral ceiling, high-end appliances, quartz counter tops, Jacuzzi, tiled glass shower, barn doors, etc.)

Exit Strategy: Stage property and take distinct pictures including 3D with drone technology and list property for sale.

5. The Cosmetic Fixer Upper: These properties require mostly slight improvements—paint touchups, drywall repairs, floor refinishing. It might also include lighting fixtures, doors, window shutters.

The formula for the Cosmetic Fixer Upper:

THE COSMETIC FIXER UPPER
   PROPERTY ANALYSIS
   Formula for Cosmetic Fixer Upper

Property Values   _____

Property Asking Price   _____

SUBTRACT:

Cosmetic estimates (Paint, carpet, etc.)   _____

Closing costs   _____

Advertising,   _____

Miscellaneous   _____

Your offer (include closing costs)   _____

DETERMINE:

PITI (Principal, Interest Taxes,
   Insurance) Investor's Monthly
   Payment*   _____

Rent In Area (Consult Rentometer)†   _____

Gross Monthly Rent   _____

Cash Flow Strategy: With this strategy, you buy the property, might need carpet and paint, clean up the property, and put it back on the market for rent.

What is the advantage?

You own the property and the tenant is paying for your property and you take advantage of all the tax benefits that comes with investment property ownership.

Appreciation: Over time the property should increase in value.

If you should refinance, you will be able to take out equity and, because it is borrowed money, you don't have to pay taxes on the money.

A CASE STUDY

With limited inventory you can work with investors to create inventories:

GAV Capital Partners LLC have partnered with investors to buy-rehab or buy and tear down and build new construction.

I help my investors locate and buy these properties through my network of wholesale investors.

---

* Subtract rent in area from investor's monthly mortgage payment equals gross monthly rent.

† Rentometer is a site that gives users an estimate of what rent prices are in the nearby vicinity of a subject property.

I provide marketing, sales, and all advisory services. I help my investors decide the kind of homes to build, the price point, how to market the houses, and I also serve as the listing agent.

A case in point: We have a property under contract to close—the deal is a tear down. I found the property through one of my wholesale investors.

Here are the numbers:

Purchase and soft cost = $169,000
Construction funds from Hard Money Lender = $250,000
Total purchase and construction = $419,000
After Repair Value (ARV) = $675,000
Total gross profit: $675,000 - $419,000 = $256,000
Front End Commission on the deal is 169,000 x 0.3% = $5,070
Back End Listing to Sell at $675,000 x 0.4% = $27,000
Total Gross Commission = $32,070

Recommended Reading

Recommended Real Estate Books

1. *How I Turned $1,000 into Five Million in Real Estate in My Spare Time* by William Nickerson
2. *Building Wealth One House at a Time: Making it Big on Little Deals* by John W. Schaub
3. *Keys To Investing in Real Estate* by Jack P. Friedman and Jack C. Harris
4. *Keys To Buying Foreclosed and Bargain Homes* by Jack P. Friedman and Jack C Harris
5. *Making Big Money in Real Estate Without Tenants, Banks, or Rehab Projects* by Peter Conti and David Finkel
6. *How To Borrow Your Way to Real Estate Riches* by Tyler Hicks
7. *Wealth 101* by Wade Cook
8. *How To Make Big Money in Real Estate* by Tyler Hicks
9. *The Millionaire Mind* by Thomas J Stanley PhD.
10. *The Book on Rental Property Investing* by Brandon Turner (of BiggerPockets)
11. *Hidden Fortunes* by Albert J. Lowry PhD

E-Books Real Estate Investment Books by George Ansong

1. *Beginners Guide to Real Estate Investing*
2. *Wholesaling 101 — The Street-Smart Guide to Wholesaling*
3. *Borrow Your Way to Real Estate Riches*
4. *Creative Real Estate Financing*

To download these books, visit www.thecashflowrealestateagent.com

50 Websites That Will Post Listings for Free

1. Craigslist

Craigslist often comes to mind first among free online marketplaces. As one of the world's highest-traffic websites, that should be no surprise. Craigslist has long been an ideal place to find buyers and sellers for all types of real estate, mainly because scores of people take part in every subcategory of this platform. Craigslist ads are no-frills, which follow the website's general theme.

2. Zillow

Another massive platform, it's the number one marketplace for buyers and sellers of real estate. Zillow is one of a few that allow property owners to post sale-by-owner listings for free. This is a big deal.

3. Facebook

In addition to being the dominant player in social media, it has grown into an effective place to buy and sell real estate. Whether you post properties for sale in the Facebook Marketplace or a "For Sale" Facebook group in your area, there are tons of opportunities for more exposure.

4. Connected Investor

A sizable online community of like-minded people. The site offers more than just networking opportunities; you can also list your properties for sale (as well as view properties for sale from other investors). The vast majority of folks on this website are real estate investors; therefore, properties usually won't be priced absurdly high but, instead, for investors who want to squeeze some equity out of the deal.

5. ForSaleByOwner

A site for property owners who want to sell their homes without paying an agent commission. Ironically, both of their premium listing packages involve third-party agents who get paid by the buyer or the seller. However, the most significant feature of this site is its free thirty-day listing option. The site's ads are put together pretty nicely too.

6. LetGo

This site seems to prioritize the ease-of-use and visual elements of each listing. My interactions with the website show that it appears to be intended for a mobile audience than those using desktop computers.

7. Fizber

Another helpful website for listing properties; it's a key platform with a targeted audience for real estate buyers. Fizber also offers sellers the ability to list their properties on the MLS for a flat fee (without signing a contract with a real estate agent), a notable feature that most real estate listing sites don't bring to the table.

8. Oodle

Oodle probably has the most streamlined process for posting a property for sale. You don't have to navigate through page after page of details, sellers can fill out a straightforward submission form to get their entire listing compiled and posted in a matter of seconds. It's especially fast if you already have the listing information prepared and you're just copying it from another source.

9. Asset Column

This platform is designed pretty well, and the website as a whole looks great. It makes the process of putting together a listing very easy.

10. FindMyRoof

FindMyRoof does a pretty decent job of putting together a nice listing that gives all the basic details in an easy-to-follow format. It's not a complex process to create a listing, and the site doesn't draw in a huge amount of traffic, but it is a relatively targeted audience of real estate buyers, which may make the site worth your time and consideration.

11. HotPads

Hotpads is unique on this list because it's only intended for listing properties (houses, apartments, condos, etc.) for rent, not for sale. Nevertheless, this still fills a significant need for many property owners. Because it's one of the more prominent players, with a well-designed layout and interface, it's worth mentioning. This site pulls in over ten million monthly visitors, and as one of the Zillow group brands, all listings are syndicated to appear on Zillow and Trulia, which is a huge value add.

12. Cozy

This site, too, is intended only for rental properties and markets them to prospective tenants. Also, prospective tenants do not search Cozy for rental properties—instead, Cozy syndicates their listings to websites like Realtor and Doorsteps. Cozy is one of the few sites—maybe the only one—that allows independent landlords to get their rental listings on the MLS via Realtor.com.

13. Kahping

Kahping makes it very easy to create real estate listings, add photos, and highlight what the features and details are of each new listing (and it does a better job than some of the nonspecialized websites like Craigslist). The listings make pretty good use of space, giving users different tabs to click on and expand to see more information.

14. AdLandPro

Users can post free classified ads, local classifieds, and do free online promotions with online business ads or classified postings.

15. BuyandSell

BuyandSell is a free listing site that was launched in 2005 in Toronto, Canada. The site serves users in more than 190 countries and six continents, focusing on accelerating trade between buyers and sellers in every market across the globe.

16. ClassifiedAds

Another free listing website with a similar look and feel to Craigslist. You aren't required to maintain an account here, and the ads on this site also come with a nice little inquiry form at the bottom of each listing—so it's one less step for an interested party to contact the seller for more information. The listings also allow sellers to link to third-party websites, which is a nice extra feature to send more traffic to your selling website.

17. FreeClassifieds

FreeClassifieds is another website you can use to sell pretty much anything. You can post and search local classified ads.

18. WebClassifieds

WebClassifieds is another US-based classified ad website you can use to buy, sell, or trade. This is another catch-all platform that is used to sell all types of items.

19. LandSaleListings

LandSaleListings is a great site to know about if you're trying to list and sell vacant land. The site offers a few paid listing options, but it also allows users to post free listings, but with only one picture. It's not necessarily the most versatile or beautifully designed site on this list, but it's another valid option that doesn't cost anything and can potentially get your ad seen by a new audience.

20. AdsGlobe

AdsGlobe is an advertising gateway for online classifieds in jobs, real estate, rentals, autos, services, items for sale, travel, events, pets, business, and community.

21. Beycome

Beycome is a real estate listing site that offers both free and paid listing options. It's designed specifically with FSBO sellers in mind.

22. Hoobly

Hoobly is a pretty sizable, classified ad platform that draws in millions of visitors per month. People use this site to sell arts, books, clothing, electronics, home and garden, pets, real estate, vehicles, and more.

23. PennySaverUSA

PennySaverUSA is another run-of-the-mill classified ad site where you can browse and post free online listings, get coupons, and find other interesting deals.

24. Claz.org

The claim behind Claz.org is that you can search all classified ad sites at once. Given that you can also post ads for free, it's probably worth checking out.

25. Recycler

Recycler is another online marketplace that connects buyers and sellers at the local level. It's an ideal platform for buying and selling cars, pets, real estate, jobs, and more.

26. REIFreeClassifieds

This site is geared toward the real estate investing industry; it's not just a catch-all listing site that anyone can use for purposes unrelated to real estate. If you're looking to tap into a bit more of a focused audience, this one could be a great fit.

27. Geebo

Geebo is a website where it's easy to place ads and safer to search. As stated on its home page, the company's goal is to go the extra mile to help build, protect, and connect communities.

28. AmericanListed

AmericanListed provides millions of safe and local classifieds for jobs, rentals, pets, housing, real estate, cars, boats, services, events, clothing, furniture, and motorcycles.

29. FreeAdsCity

FreeAdsCity is a photo classifieds site that lets you post and browse classified ads under auto, real estate, pets, furniture, electronics, and more.

30. FreeAdsTime

A worldwide classified ads website where you can browse and post ads with a photo. Categories include houses and apartments for rent, roommates, local jobs, pets, vehicles, and other items.

31. BeatYourPrice

BeatYourPrice is another standard classified ad website to browse and post listings, including categories such as art, electronics, jobs, real estate, jobs, and more.

32. Loot

Loot is a pretty well-designed listing website to post real estate ads and browse the site for other opportunities, such as jobs, cars, properties, pets, services, and more.

33. EPage

EPage was one of the first "dot-com" companies globally, founded in 1994 as an "internet-only" business dedicated to providing the best classified and auction services to its customers. The EPage network has more than 850,000 monthly visitors and has displayed more than three billion classified advertisements.

34. DomesticSale

DomesticSale is a place where you can post US-based online classified ads. Use this place to buy and sell autos, real estate, or general merchandise.

35. Locanto

Locanto is a user-to-user local community classifieds site. You can use the site to post and search ads, find a new place to live, buy a new car, find a job, and more.

36. AdPost

AdPost is another classified ad listing website that can be used to browse and sell all the major categories you'd expect to see on a classified ad website.

37. Kugli

Kugli is a classified ad site and international business networking site. They have dedicated categories for dozens of different local and regional classified ads.

38. SalesSpider

A social network designed to help small to midsize businesses expand their networks, connect with contracting and supplier opportunities, post free classified ads, and gain free access to sales leads and business opportunities. It's supposedly one of the largest free social networks for business owners and includes sales leads and prospect lists, classified ads, business directories, and business forums.

39. Ablewise

Ablewise is one of the biggest business ad-posting sites that lets you post such ads as rentals, automobiles, business opportunities, merchandise, services, employment, and more.

40. BuySellCommunity

BuySellCommunity is an online community where you can buy and sell your stuff and open your own online storefront.

41. House.Info

House.Info is one of the few websites on this list that focuses on real estate. The site features thousands of listings and brings in a fair number of monthly visitors—so this one could be of interest for the specific purpose of posting your properties for sale.

42. Gold Classifieds

GoldClassifieds provides online classifieds, advertising services, and is available for global users.

43. AdFreePosting

AdFreePosting is another classified ad listing website that can be used to browse and sell all the major categories you'd expect to see.

44. FreeToClassifieds

FreeToClassifieds appears to be a pretty basic listing website, but it could do the trick. This platform will allow you to publish real estate listings without an account.

45. TopClassifieds

TopClassifieds is another basic classified listing site. Nothing particularly special about it—another platform to get some extra exposure for your listings.

46. AdsKeep

AdsKeep is another basic (and relatively unsophisticated)

classified listing site. This site has several real estate-related categories and could be a good place to connect with buyers and sellers.

47. SuperAds

SuperAds is a pretty self-explanatory classified ads website. If you know how to use Craigslist, you should figure this one out pretty quickly.

48. Global Free Classified Ads

As the name implies, Global Free Classified Ads features listings worldwide, so it's not the most centralized place to connect with local buyers and sellers. However, if you're looking for more of a global audience, it could be a good fit.

49. 10DayAds

10DayAds is a place to sell new or used items and listing your business in the US or worldwide, enabling you to reach millions of potential buyers. There is a real estate category available, along with the other standard categories.

50. HouseList

HouseList has a fairly small audience, and the website doesn't have the freshest design or layout, but its audience is specifically targeted in the real estate space—so it could be a great place to post your listing.

My Observation

I think you should advertise your properties to anybody, even if it's just a handful of people—especially when there's no cost to you.

About the Author

George Ansong is a real estate guru, realtor, entrepreneur, investor, teacher, lecturer, coach, and mentor.

George Ansong is the ultimate entrepreneur. Starting as a cab driver in the early 1970s in New York City, he discovered his passion for real estate investing by attending a "No Money Down" seminar and met his mentor, Tyler Hicks, of International Wealth Success fame. Mr. Ansong bought his first property in Brooklyn, a multiunit property that he later sold. He then bought a few properties in the Jersey City area before moving to Atlanta with his family in 1990s.

Mr. Ansong bought and sold a few businesses, and with this knowledge in real estate, began investing. He also started teaching real estate investment courses at area colleges, including Kennesaw State University, Chattahoochee Technical Institute, and Perimeter College. As an adjunct instructor, Mr. Ansong wrote all his instructional manuals, which are now e-books on various topics on real estate investment.

He later formed a company, Quadrant Investments LLC, with his partner, Jeff Cohen. They bought and sold more than $50 million worth of real estate with his front money partners before the market crashed in 2008. Mr. Ansong obtained his real estate license in 2000. He worked as agent for Property Systems of Georgia, one of the leading foreclosure real estate brokerage companies in the Southeast, where his focus was working with real estate investors.

During this time, Mr. Ansong was still teaching, conducting

seminars, and organizing real estate field trips for his students. He later worked for Prudential Georgia Realty, now Berkshire Hathaway HomeServices. Currently, Mr. Ansong is a realtor with Maximum One Realty in Atlanta. His specialty lies in working with real estate investors. His company, GAV Capital Partners LLC, works with investors providing consulting and strategic direction to numerous investors who are involved in rehabbing properties in the metro Atlanta area. Currently, he also teaches an online course, "Buy-Fix-Flip," for REI-USA—www.rei-usa.com. Mr. Ansong is a graduate of Bernard M. Baruch College of the City University of New York (CUNY) with a degree in business administration. His hobbies include reading, traveling, and listening to music.

www.ingramcontent.com/pod-product-compliance
Lightning Source LLC
Chambersburg PA
CBHW070714130626
46553CB00005B/1991